God's Presence in Light of Satan

Connie Ray Coats, Sr.

PublishAmerica
Baltimore

First printing

ISBN: 1-60474-814-1
PUBLISHED BY PUBLISHAMERICA, LLLP
www.publishamerica.com
Baltimore

Printed in the United States of America

DEDICATION

First of all, I dedicate this book to God. Without Him, it couldn't have been written.

Second, I dedicate it to my mom (Latrell Tones) and grandmother (Rosa Tones) who planted a seed in me at my early age knowing that one day it would blossom.

Third, I would like to dedicate it to all of the lost souls that God sent by me to give me testimonies of their hurts. Hopefully I was able to pour a little water on their deep-hidden seeds.

Last, I would like to dedicate this book to the future readers of this book with high hopes that my stories will bring them closer to God. Realizing that I can't save anyone, nor can I take them with me to Heaven, I can write of my personal experiences and maybe God will use one word, one story, one scripture, to get the readers to give Him a chance. If I went through the stories, then someone else is going through the same and prayerfully, God will lead them to this book letting them know they're not alone. I praise God for sending me through all that He did because it made me a stronger person, a wiser person, a more spiritual person who looks at people through a spiritual eye instead of fleshly eye. It made me a more humble person, a more caring person, a more patient person. I have a stronger faith/belief in God. I am able to maybe help someone else's hurt, and most of all, I love and trust God more than I did before. It is totally a fact that "greater is He that's in me, than he that's in the world!"

CHAPTER ONE

Earlier Experiences with God

A: GRANDMOTHER'S FAITH

During the earlier years of my life, I was blessed with this grandmother we called Mama Tones. She was a devout Christian and loved God more than anything or anyone else. She believed in God, family, and love in that order. She was an old woman who carried herself as a Christian, no matter where she went. We didn't have much, but she depended on God to *supply all of her needs.* I don't believe I ever saw Mama Tones worry about food, money, etc., and if she did, she didn't show it. She would whip us when we were bad and love us when we were good, thus making us better people. She prayed day and night for all of us; then, you would hear her sing one of those old Negro hymns "Jesus Keep Me Near the Cross" or "God Will Make a Way Somehow." Her husband was killed in a rodeo years earlier, so I never got the pleasure of knowing him. She wouldn't talk about him very much for some reason and we didn't question her.

I remembered her loving to cook those Sunday meals and invite the preacher over to eat after church service. We had to be on our best behavior when he came over or we'd have serious consequences after he left.

Anytime the church doors were open, Mama Tones would be there on her front row seat. She insisted that we were there also, without excuse. No matter what we did on Saturday night, we were required to get our white shirt ready and go to church on time the following Sunday morning. At one time, I was elected choir director and remember that the first song I directed was "What Is This." All we would see during service was Mama Tones and all the others just rock back and forth with one hand held to the sky. The older congregation wouldn't say a word, but just rock until our little short preacher would tear down the house with the word. The services were so "spirit-filled" sometimes the old men and women would get up and dance. That was the first time I really knew that there was something incredible all around us. Even then, at this young age, I felt different inside although I didn't understand what was happening to me. I now understand what those 120 people felt when the Holy Spirit came down on each of them making them talk in their own language.

I remember vividly Mama Tones telling me that one day I would become a preacher, not understanding that all she was doing was planting a seed. The Bible tells us that *a good fruit tree cannot bear bad fruits* and I know that Mama Tones was a good fruit tree. She demanded respect and from kids to stay in their places. When a group of adults were gathered talking, all she would have to do to us was look at us with a frown. That told us not to come in there nor say a word while we were leaving out to play. This is very unlike today when adults allow kids to sit in their conversations or talk to them any kind of way. Even if the neighbors complained to her about our badness, she would tell them to whip us, then, when we got home, she would do the same. She would definitely not spare the rod, but it taught us respect. I know I wasn't an angel and throughout all the badness I did, I never got into serious trouble. I realize now that Mama Tones was always interceding to God to have mercy on me and keep me under His protection. When she died, part of me died with her and there is no doubt in my mind that she went home to live with God and one day I'll see her again.

B: MOTHER'S BELIEF

My mom was a good lady named Latrell. She cleaned houses for a living to provide the best care she could for us. She wasn't as religious as my grandmother, yet she believed strongly in God. One of my brothers was handicapped (couldn't talk or use his limbs properly) and my mother took complete care of him. Back in those days, the mothers of a handicapped child thought it was only their responsibility to raise him/her the best they could without help from neighbors, government, or anyone else.

I don't know whether it was because of shame or not, but it certainly wasn't regret. I know she had to get her strength from God because He was the only One who could keep her going.

She enjoyed going to the juke joints with her favorite girlfriend and drinking beer. She didn't make very much money, yet we never did without. She was the only woman I knew who could take a pound of ground beef, stretch it enough to feed all of us, the neighbor kids, and whoever stopped by. This reminds me of the times Jesus took two fish and five loaves of bread and fed the multitude with baskets left over. There's one thing Jesus did that my mother always did, that was to bless the food first before eating. My mother also liked to dress nice and even with all of her other obligations, God provided her with nice clothes. Back in those days, the businesses allowed credit to its customers because everyone knew everybody.

The year before my graduation of high school, my mother got married and she and my handicapped brother moved to Houston Texas. I realized that God had provided that break for her because my stepfather provided totally for her and my brother. The only house she had to clean was her own. She was not worried about where the money for bills was going to come from, and she could take care of my brother full-time. That was nothing less than a blessing from God. *Come to me all ye who labor with a heavy-laden and I'll give you rest.*

I also remember when my parents were struggling with

their financial obligations and didn't know where to turn. God took my older brother home to Heaven and my mom received $10,000 from his insurance policy. God said He would supply all of our needs. I remember many times I would see my mother come in from cleaning two or three houses in one day so tired she didn't know what to do. Even then, she would still fix dinner if my grandmother didn't and take care of my brother. Before she died, she would always say she was so tired she wished she would just lie down and not wake up. God must have heard her prayer because the evening she died, she told her husband that she was very tired and she was going to lie down to get her a little rest. She did and never woke back up. When I was preparing to bury my mother, the insurance policies totaled $2,000 less than the amount I needed. I didn't want to ask for donations from family because I didn't want to be ashamed nor did I have the money. God heard my cry and had my job give me all of the time off I needed with pay and also give me the rest of the money needed to bury my mother. Also about ten of my fellow employees along with the president and his wife attended the funeral to give me moral support. Even through my mom's drunkenness, God still heard her prayers and had mercy on her.

C: DISCRIMINATION

Back in those days, many people spoke about

discrimination among themselves, but we still had to live through it. I remember going through back doors because we weren't allowed to go through the front ones. I remember having to drink out of the "blacks only" water fountains along with going to an all-black school. We'd look at how the whites lived and only wished we had the opportunity to live that way. We as blacks would stay on our part of town and the whites would do the same. I worked for this heavyset white man named Mr. Greer who would blow a whistle every morning for me to come to work. It was degrading work but the few cents he paid me taught me the value of working hard. He would have me feed his livestock, drive him around town on his time, even wash his feet and clip his toenails while he spit all over the place. He would make his wife cry all of the times for no reason. Sure there had to be a God somewhere? I'm sure many blacks wondered why God allowed this division especially when we were all His children. Although we had come a long way from the slavery days, it still seemed so unfair just because of the color of our skin. We knew no other way of life, so we just had to pray and bear it. At that time we didn't know that God was sending a Martin Luther King, Rosa Parks, and all of the other great black leaders to stand up when we were too afraid. *When you've done all that you can, just stand.*

Around 1967 we found out that our all-black school would be integrated. It finally seemed that equality was just a little closer. We must remember that many didn't like Jesus but that didn't stop Him from trying to get people to change their beliefs. He was laughed at, tortured, denied by the closest ones to Him like Peter, and endured more suffering than we could ever experience all the way to His death. Even until the end, He asked God to forgive them for they knew not what they did. The question becomes, can we forgive all those that did us wrong?

D: IMAGINATION OF GOOD LIFE

I remember I used to look in magazines, see the big two-story houses, see the nice cars, etc., and pray that one day God would bless me with those things. My mom bought me this toy cash register with toy currency and I used to act like I was selling merchandise to invisible customers. I would make steering wheels out of coat hangers and run around making believe I was driving expensive cars. I was very good in school, especially excelling in math, English, reading, and hoping one day I would be able to use those talents landing a good job. I didn't consider going to college because we didn't have the money nor did we know anything about grants, scholarships, etc. All I knew was that my hometown didn't offer me a future that interested me and I had to leave. About three to five hours after I got my diploma, I left town with relatives and went to San Antonio, Texas. Abraham just left not knowing where he was going and left his kindred behind. He just had faith in God and knew that everything would be fine.

CHAPTER TWO

Leaving Home with Satan

A: FAMILY CULTS

Upon arrival in San Antonio, I moved in with my aunt until I could get out on my own. Although there was belief in God in the house, no one practiced daily walking with Him. The only time a church visit was done was during a funeral, wedding, or various other holidays. Almost each weekend the family would get together, play games, get drunk, and talk about the people my family didn't like. The Bible says *judge not* but we didn't listen. Even though we knew it was wrong, there was always one old aunt that the family agreed with and looked up to. Each Sunday we would eat a good home-cooked meal, yet there was never a *blessing* of the food. Now all of us had a godly seed planted in us growing up, yet we overlooked it because it was more fun serving Satan. Most people think by serving God, you lose all of your fun in life. They think it's boring and you have to close yourself up into this shell, afraid to do/say anything. You can't sing a song, can't dance, can't discuss anything but the Bible, etc. It's not the beat of the music, but the lyrics that are sung in the songs. It's not the dance steps, yet the seductiveness added to the steps with seductive music. There's nothing wrong with discussing current events or other things. It's when we include the profanity, rumors, selfishness, etc., with our conversations. We will have more joy when we include God in our conversations and possibly understand them more. Jesus said if we are ashamed of Him, then He'll be ashamed of us to His Father. By including Him, you'll hesitate or think before you say something. How many times have unsaved people said, "Excuse me" to saved people after they've cursed, etc., during a good conversation? The church house doesn't make the church, the people do and assembly is necessary. People tell you all of the time, "I go to church every Sunday," yet they go back to their ungodly ways right after they leave the building. Something is wrong with that church because when God is involved, changes have to happen. These people came out the same old way they went in.

B: ODD JOB SECURITY

A little later it was time for me to seek employment. I went through a variety of odd jobs that didn't satisfy my needs. I was bored with the government job, couldn't stand the smell at the fish restaurant, thought I was too good for the sewer survey job, and thought there was no future at the plumbers' warehouse job. I was very good at all of those jobs, yet I felt this void for whatever reason. I didn't know if it was because there were not enough people to interact with on each of the jobs or whether another future was destined for me. Finally, a secretary from the plumbing job had a son who managed a major grocery store and set me up with a job with him. I was very happy and I guess it stemmed from my childhood interest in the toy cash register. I stayed there for a long time and worked myself up from produce clerk to opening/closing the entire store. I was also the only black with that much control in that area. God knew what my desire was and He placed that secretary in my path. He said He'd give us the desires of our hearts. When He allowed me to get the toy cash register, He knew then that job was being held for me and that I would learn different cultures and how to carry myself with all kinds of people. He was also teaching me how the upper class of people lived for future references.

C: WEAKNESSES EXPOSED BY SATAN

Everything in my life was, I thought, beginning to look up for me. I had a good job, making a little money, and even started buying my first home. I even transferred from the north side of town to the east side to be closer to home. The east side was predominantly black but I soon realized that the older blacks were cautious of the young smart blacks who wanted to get ahead. It was as though they were jealous and threatened of their own positions. I was very good at my job, even running two cash registers at the same time, keeping the customer lines moving. The more noticeable it had become, the more difficult my black store manager was making my job. It had gotten so bad that on New Year's Eve when he needed all of the employees he could get, I walked in and quit.

During this time, Satan knew all of my weaknesses (alcohol, night clubs, and different women) and knew I wasn't walking with God. That made it easier to take advantage of my situation. I loved the high the alcohol gave me. It removed the shyness and made me brave to approach situations I wouldn't have normally faced. My problem was when I started drinking. I didn't know how to stop, especially on weekends. I used to buy a half gallon of gin and my friend and I would drink about three fourths of that then buy a bottle of white wine to refill the bottle. Each morning during my hangover I would use the famous words most all drunks use, "Lord, if you let me get over this one, I won't do it again." Of course, I lied to the Lord because as the day went on and I felt better, later that evening I'd start again. I loved going to the clubs and had a different club each night of the week. I had to dress nice for each visit and spent lots of my money on new matching outfits. After the clubs in town would close at 2 a.m., I used to go to this after-hour club that stayed open all night. I never had to worry about not having liquor because they would sell me a bottle under the table at the after-hour club. I loved to dance and find new women to take home with me. I thought I had it really going on, not knowing I was completely in Satan's grips.

The alcohol, clubs, and women were my gods failing to remember that God said there would be no other god before Him. Satan will make you feel you're on top of the world when you are actually on top of destruction. He makes you feel the good times will last forever. Satan doesn't want you to live for the future, yet day to day. He tells you if you lose this job, you can always get another one. He tells you to go ahead and spend your bill money on liquor, clothes, clubs, etc., you'll get paid next week, then you can catch up. He tells you to call in sick at the job because you haven't missed that many days and your boss will understand. He tells you that each new woman looks a little better than the ones you are currently seeing, and the more the merrier. Satan totally has you "confused" because he is the author of confusion. He'll never tell you the whole story, only enough to keep you believing that you're happy.

There were many incidents that happened that I felt at the time that "Mr. Luck" or "close call" was on my side because I never should've walked away from them. Below are some examples.

One night I got so drunk I passed out in the middle of a busy expressway. I was in the middle lane, car still running, lights still on, about 3 a.m. All it took was an eighteen-wheeler or another vehicle to hit my car and most likely, kill me. I woke up to a police car's flashing lights. He pushed me over to a safe location with his car and allowed me to sleep my drunkenness off until I was able to drive home. Not only should I have been killed, the least I should've been was taken to jail for DWI.

One evening I was drinking and driving when I was stopped by a police officer. The cup of alcohol was in a holder hung on my car door. When he asked me if I had been drinking, I told him yes and opened my door. When I did, some of the drink spilled out of the cup, which he saw. I exited the car because I just knew I would be arrested for DWI. To my surprise, that officer just told me to be careful and allowed me to continue my journey. He should've arrested me or at the least, made me pour out all of my drinks including the almost full liquor bottle, or made someone else in the car drive. That officer had to have known that I was drunk, if no more, he should have smelled the liquor on my breath.

Many times we would be so drunk around 4 a.m. that we would decide to drive to my hometown, which was about a hundred miles from where we were. We'd have the blues blasting, still drinking, driving fast, singing, and having no idea of the danger we were placing other drivers and ourselves in. There were many steep hills to quick corners on many stretches of that highway that would surprise you during the day, let alone at night. There were livestock and deer crossings on those dark country roads that should have been a fear to us, but they weren't. All of those times, which were many, we made it to our destination without a single incident. When you start drinking alcohol around 6 p.m. and continue until around 4 a.m., you definitely shouldn't been driving a vehicle. Not only was I putting my life in jeopardy, but all of the people who were riding with me. If livestock or deer would've jumped in front of us, if I would've missed one of those quick curves, if I would've met another vehicle facing me at the top of one of those hills, if I would've just lost control while pouring another drink or changing the music, etc., with the fast speed I was driving, there is no doubt in my mind, all of us would've been killed.

One night I met this girl who lived in one of the most crime-infiltrated projects in the city. When I first arrived in town after graduation, I was told never to go into that community because of the drugs, killings, etc. That didn't stop me because of the hunger I had for different women and a certain one who lived there fit all of my requirements. One night when we were in bed with my gun close to me, her roommate or her roommate's boyfriend came into the apartment. At that moment, I felt that there was going to be a shootout or some other trouble because I didn't know if it was his bed I was in. I really didn't know her and wondered if it was a setup or if it was her unexpected husband/boyfriend coming home. She just said nothing as this guy peeped in the room we were in, then he turned around and walked out of the apartment. She finally told me he was a relative, but that could never be verified, so I just forgot about the incident. This was the first time anything like that had ever happened to me and even though there was a chance of repeat, I continued seeing that same woman.

Satan doesn't care what situation he puts us in. He will put the exact type of woman/man we, not God, dream of right in front of us just to keep us serving him. We don't see or think clearly when we're in a drunken state and that's where Satan wants to keep us.

This guy walked in, surveyed all of the rooms including ours, then turned around and walked out. He could've come in and shot up the place because he apparently had his own key. If I hadn't been drunk, I probably wouldn't have placed myself in that dangerous position.

Drugs never really interested me, yet I tried the marijuana and pills. The marijuana made me feel like I couldn't breathe so I left it alone. One night I took this pill called a "red" and it made me so high that I stayed up for about three days in a row. I couldn't come down no matter what I tried. I couldn't go to sleep and the only thing I could do was walk back and forth. While in that state of mind, I asked God to take the highness away and if He did, I'd never knowingly swallow that kind of pill again. I couldn't imagine how anyone would want to be in that condition for consecutive days, yet there are crackheads that are. I can't even remember the names of the people I got that pill from, but I know I was drunk when I accepted it. Those drugs could've killed me because I didn't really know the people I got them from. I met them in the streets and allowed peer pressure to get to me. Peer pressure is a weakness that Satan preys on because most times, if not all of the times, he's the one who puts the peers in our presence. The ones who gave me the pill could've been serial killers who got their kicks off of these sort of deaths. We need to be very familiar with the people we hang around and associate with, especially when we accept things from them. Normally, when people use prescribed drugs consistently, they are trying to hide a hurt deep inside their soul they feel man cannot heal. They feel that staying high all of the time covers the hurt and gives them a sense of belonging like all others who, in their minds, are happy. They feel that's the only way they can fit in and be happy also. They walk around thinking they're alive, not knowing their souls are dead.

The above examples are a fraction of the many things that happened that should've resulted in death, yet didn't. I even lost my house because of my drinking and partying behaviors. The above show that even with me serving Satan so completely, God was still watching over me. He was the One who pulled me out of those bad situations just in time and protected me. It was just like God told Satan about Job that he could try him, but he just couldn't kill him. We feel like we are "lucky" when we escape badness, but when we're truly walking with God or those things interfere with God's purpose, there is no such thing as luck. God knows our futures and His plan must be fulfilled. He allows things to happen to us just to get our attention and hopefully give our lives to Him. He also brings us out so we can tell our testimony to someone He sends our way in the future who is going through the same thing we went through. That way we can give them a personal account of getting through and God will get all of the praise.

Many of us would rather not remember, but we can't be selfish, yet help someone else with our experience, even if it opens hurtful wounds. If we can't help others, even opening our past, God should've allowed us to die because not helping, we're dead already.

D: FIRST MARRIAGE

A few months later, things began to look up for me after moving back with my aunt. I had gotten another job and because of my previous experience, I was hired into a management position. I also slowed down on going to the clubs and drinking every night, but I made up for all of it on the weekends. Friday nights after work I'd pick up my partner and we would party until the early morning hours. We would go to sleep, wake up, clean my car, mix our drinks, then, ride around each Saturday afternoon through neighborhoods to find new women.

One Saturday afternoon while driving through this neighborhood, I drove by my first cousin's house. This short, dark-skinned, shapely woman with this large afro was outside visiting with my cousin. I stopped and introduced myself to this woman and gave her my phone number. We got to know each other and started dating after she moved down here from another state; she was only visiting her brother when I first met her. After a while seeing that all of my family liked her and her family liked me, we got married. She already had a little girl from a previous relationship, which didn't matter to me because if you accept the mother, you have to take the kids also. Even though both of us had good jobs, had moved into a rented house, and began a life together, I still didn't give up my partying. In fact I got very drunk at my bachelor party the night before my wedding and the next day I was late getting to the church. I was still in the tub when I should've been standing in front of the preacher. During the ceremony after I finally arrived still hung over from the night before, the preacher mixed up our names. I was still allowing Satan to control my life even as God was allowing me to rebound from my earlier disasters. Satan knew I liked to drink alcohol and chase women so he kept the liquor available. He also will put women in your path just the way I liked them because he knew it wouldn't take a long time to get to know them. By my not getting strength from God, Satan knew that was one of my weaknesses. You make wrong decisions because here's this woman you've dreamed of and you will not let her get away. Satan will also make them tell you everything he know you want to hear even if you believe it's too good to be true. Even though Satan will set us up for a future destruction, God will allow signs to appear before our eyes, giving us a choice to stop or go forward. Most always we elect to go forward and ignore the obvious signs because it seems easier to handle. I should've realized there was something wrong by all of the bad things that occurred all the way up to our vows. I should've known that Satan had control over this marriage. We still hung together, trying to make our marriage work but it was hard balancing because of my drinking problem. She began to follow me when I went out but I had it set up at each regular club that when my wife drove up in front, I would be let out of the back door.

Just before the end of our marriage, my older brother came to our home for a visit. He and I had just gotten very close as brothers mainly because he had been in the military our earlier years. That day he got sick, I rushed him to the hospital, and a few weeks later, he was dead. It was devastating to me and especially my wife because those two had also gotten very close. The only thing that helped me was my aunt telling me during one of my private crying spells, "God won't put more on you than you can bear." I'll always remember those words. Later, God blessed us with a healthy baby boy (seems like He was replacing the void I had for my brother). Things continued on a downward spiral even with our newborn who was named after me. Couples who try to stay together because of the kids are only fooling themselves. All you do is put the kids in "choosing positions" that is very uncomfortable for them. They will get over the separation much easier and sooner rather than seeing the deteriorating distance happening between the couple. Kids don't make a marriage, true love between the couple does. There are many couples who don't have God in their lives are trying to stay together just to keep the kids with a mother and father under the same roof. All they do is hurt the kids more. A house divided cannot stand.

Our marriage hit the fan one Mother's Day weekend when I agreed to meet my mom in our hometown. My wife wouldn't go which was very odd because she'd always follow me everywhere, especially out of town. Before I left, I was going to deposit my check into our joint account, yet something came up each time I tried to do so keeping me from depositing it. I went anyway and while visiting my mother, my wife would call every day seemingly for no reason. I questioned the frequent calls because she had never done that before, but just erased it from my mind. Early afternoon at the end of my visit, I told my mother I was leaving because I wanted to get home before dark. As I headed out, I ran into some old schoolmates and decided to spend some time with them before leaving town. Finally after some hours I left, arrived home, and found this huge rock at the entrance of my front door. I felt something was wrong and found out when I walked into the house. My wife had left me, took my six-month-old son, and removed everything from our three-bedroom house except this old green hard sofa, a few eating utensils, and a few other household items. I was devastated and called my mom telling her what had happened. She told me it was fine because my wife would never enjoy all that she took because it wasn't what she took, yet how she took it.

Many days afterward I would sit on that old sofa, go to work, and get more depressed. This went on for a few months until one day I decided the world didn't owe me anything and to get up and start living again. So I moved out of the house, got an apartment, and started my life back over. My wife had gone out of state to her hometown, put all of our furniture into a storage unit in my city until she got settled, and didn't call or write for years. The only time I heard from her was when she filed for child support and tried to make me pay for another child she birthed out of state. The only reason I didn't have to pay for the other child was because when my attorney general rep called New Orleans' rep, she was put on hold and that made her mad. She hung up and ordered me to pay for my child only.

Things were looking up again for me with my new apartment, financially, and my retail job. The job took a lot of my time but I still found time to drink and party. They promoted me to a Supervisor over about ten stores in the worst part of town that were having serious losses. That was fine with me because then I could prove myself and every improvement I made would be very obvious. After a while, my group of stores became the best in the company and I began gaining enormous respect from my bosses.

My major faults during this time other than my personal time partying was having sexual relationships with my white female employees. Even still, I was exceeding all of the company's expectations of my stores and me. Even though I was in my mess and not doing right by my wife, God was still looking out for me. If I had been able to deposit my check, the money would've been gone because she cleaned out our account before she left. That would've left me with no money, making my problems worse. I'm almost sure God knew what was going to happen and knew I would need my check to maintain until I got paid again, so He blocked me from depositing it. I know now that the only reason for the phone calls was to make sure I was with my mother and a chance for her to schedule her move. I'm sure that God placed my friends in my path, knowing of my drunkenness, to delay me because if I would've left without stopping, I would have caught them moving. There is no question something terrible would have happened because of the state I was in, especially her taking my firstborn. God was very aware of the situation and timed it out right. God also was looking out for me when the attorney general got mad and hung up because He knew that was not my child. As far as the stored furniture, by the time my ex-wife came back to retrieve it, all of it had dampened where she was unable to use any of it. She didn't lose it because she wasn't right for leaving me, but it was the way she went about her leaving. My mom was right even before it happened. God uses others to give us messages from Him because He knows the future. Here again, God is giving me another chance improving my life, yet I'm still allowing Satan to hang around. When do we ever learn? No one could've done this but God.

E: UNKNOWN FATHER

For more than my twenty-plus years, I knew of my father but had never seen him. All I knew was that he was married, taught at a college, and lived in El Paso. He never tried to contact me and I had no way of contacting him, nor did I choose to do so.

Just before one summer I got a call from him asking me if he could stop by to see me because he was in town. I agreed and he came by with his girlfriend. We talked and agreed that I would go visit him the following summer so we could get to know each other better. Just before the summer began, I received a call from his girlfriend that my father had died and I needed to get there. I did and finally met my stepmother who didn't hesitate welcoming me into her home and treated me as her stepson. Before leaving we agreed to stay in contact with each other after giving me my father's car and some land. We remain close to this day. The purpose of my father's girlfriend to call me was because she had forged a will in my father's name thinking she and I would file against my stepmother. I refused, turning the paper over to my stepmother's lawyer, but she still received $50,000 from a policy my father named her beneficiary. The whole incident played out like we were in a soap opera, yet the best gift I got out of the whole thing was the close relationship with my stepmother. She knew of my father's extramarital activities, yet she still welcomed me into her life. She thought it was horrible for my father, who hadn't done anything for me since birth, to name his girlfriend as beneficiary to that insurance policy instead of me. But, it was already done and there was nothing either of us could do to rectify what had happened. This showed me that the generational adoption is real and someone down the line needs to end the curse.

After meeting my father for the first time and seeing his ways, I realized that I was so much like him. I believe God showed me the mirror (drinking, womanizing, sneakiness) as a warning just before he died so I could see myself through him. Unfortunately I refused to see. God gives us signs but it is up to us to acknowledge them. It also showed me to get to really know my kids in their early years and hopefully not die before that happens. Satan tried to use my father's girlfriend to lure me, using a weakness of money to hurt my stepmother, but God stepped in and opened my eyes to the girlfriend. He was protecting my stepmother because He knew she didn't deserve the consistent dishonesty, some of which she had already endured. Satan's test failed and I was blessed in the end because I remembered the honesty I learned in my earlier years. Satan had the girlfriend filled with so much envy and greed, she didn't recognize the seed that was planted in my spirit. My stepmother told me she went through that money so fast that she didn't enjoy her spending and that happened because of the way she received it.

CHAPTER THREE

Best Job, Yet Satan

A: ONE MAJOR FAULT

I was very happy with this job because it presented a homey atmosphere. I was the only black in upper management after the first one got caught stealing. Family members owned the company and some of them ran the daily operations. This gave them the flexibility to make in-house split decisions. This job fit my personal drinking habits because the management from top to bottom consistently drank. It also triggered me having relationships with two of my white female store managers and with my white female fellow supervisor. All functions organized by the company included alcoholic beverages as the initial priority. In fact, the company president and his secretary wife would make themselves drinks before they would get out of the parking lot at the end of each day. They stored their alcohol and mixers in the trunk of their car. They would take us out to dinners or other functions after work and buy us drinks until all in attendance were drunk. Later it became a daily habit for all us supervisors to go for a drink at a bar after work. Each supervisor was issued a company vehicle with free gas for personal and business use. There were quite a few auto accidents without any discipline administered to the driver even if he was guilty of the cause. The company would just give you another vehicle until your issued vehicle got fixed.

One night after drinking downtown with my fellow workers, I had to drive home in my drunken state. When I got in the car, something told me to drive the back streets, yet I decided to drive by expressway because I felt there would be fewer vehicles in my path. I felt because of the fast pace of the traffic, I would be able to get home faster and my route would be much straighter. I was wrong with my decision because I didn't realize how drunk I was. When I thought I was home free, I blacked out and ran over a barricade sitting on the side of the expressway. As soon as I realized what happened, I saw police car lights flashing behind me. They took me to jail, impounded the car, and charged me with DWI along with destruction of city property. I was placed on a two-year probation, had to make restitution, attend schooling, and I was prohibited to go to clubs or have any alcoholic beverage around me while on probation. You would think I would snap, but I just carefully and secretly went around the system.

The company went on for years with these practices, then suddenly there were cash flow problems and it was forced to sell. Many employees lost their jobs because of the ungodly practices that were allowed in the company. Satan knows the ideal situations to place in front of us knowing we are not strong enough in Christ to remove ourselves. He knew he already had most all of the people in this company serving him and that would be my desired atmosphere. Just like we disciple for God, Satan has people who disciple for him. Satan has to get permission from God on everything he does with us. He knows if he gets us comfortable with him, we would pull others to follow him also. The drinking wasn't the problem, yet the drunkenness was. Satan knows if he can get us to start and we have a weakness, then the chance of us getting drunk are stronger. He even began with the top of the company on this venture. I may not have gotten the DWI if I would've listened to my first thought, but Satan will always convince us to take the opposite just to prove his points. God allows Satan to have his way with us for so long because He knows our limits, unlike Satan. Also, God will allow us to deceive ourselves for so long and just as we think nothing can happen or we are achieving on our own, that's when He'll pull the rug from underneath us. When that happens, He wants us to turn to no other but Him. Our problem is even after God has removed the rug and we serve Him for a while, we go back to Satan as soon as we start to do better. This company would not have had to sell if management would have exchanged their practices of Satan for God. Nothing lasts when serving Satan, everything lasts when serving God.

B: NEW OWNERSHIP

The new ownership took over and switched out all upper management except my supervisors and me. I had earlier been promoted as the company's operations director. The only thing I felt was wrong with the top management was "the little clique" that would make company decisions over drinks at clubs. They would go to the bars after work on a daily basis and would come in the following day with hangover changes. My crew was making record numbers yet that seemed not to satisfy the vice president of the company. He came from our competition, hired because of being a drinking partner of the president. He wanted all of the glory without work, and wanted a director who wouldn't question him, even on bad decisions. Basically, I had to learn the job by trial and error because it seemed they were afraid to teach me anything. I didn't mind because what I would learn no one could ever take away from me. I was allowing the numbers to make my decisions for the company. Anything the president needed to know, he came to me instead of his vice president. That made me wonder many times why I wasn't considered for the vice president position. Then, the vice president wanted a "yes" man and hired his own operations director from the company he came from. They then had a real problem of what they were going to do with me. They had to make this transition a very careful process because they had no reason to replace me with him. Here's the only black employee in management, doing a great job, all the employees love him, making the company money, etc., and you want to replace him with a white guy you don't really know? So they decided to invent a position where I worked directly for the president as his advisor. I told the president that this new director wouldn't last, not because I didn't like him, but I asked, what would he bring to the table? I even gave the president a timetable for the new director's demise. This guy came in defrauding merchandise, sleeping with a company auditor, making sexual policies, demanding respect instead of earning it from store employees, hiring supervisors, keeping all kinds of operational secrets from his bosses, etc. The operations in the company soon took a complete turn for the worse. It lost an enormous amount of inventory which I had previously predicted to the president because of the bad things I had seen going on. This guy had even tried to turn my old employees against me, but all he did was turn them closer to me. They were even telling me all of the illegal things he was doing because of the disrespect they had for him and the respect they had for me. The losses got so bad that the president fired him and his crew and asked me to take that position again. I did so because of all of the unfairness the employees had already suffered.

This is just like many of our churches, the so-called holier-than-holy members have their own little clique.

They don't want to associate with the ones unlike them because they are afraid of being exposed of their inner ungodly secrets. They look down on members who don't have as much as they do or don't have a political relationship with the preacher. The preacher allows them to make church decisions whether right or wrong. The clique only gives financial support because they want political status making some preachers degrade the less fortunate members. Instead of telling them to give what they have, he/she chastises them, making them feel not good enough. They don't acknowledge when Jesus thought more of the old lady who gave all she had than the ones who gave more. What happened in the belief that God will supply all of our needs? We cannot buy our way to heaven and if we give for any reason other than our hearts, we may as well keep our money. If a preacher gets up behind the pulpit and the first thing he/she says is, "If you think your money is buying my suits," or "This money you're giving is not going to me," then you need to question where your offerings are going. The preacher is hiding something. Why would he/she be defensive from the start if the offerings are being spent toward the church's needs only? The preacher also relies only on information from the clique rather than all of his/her members. These preachers become no better than the clique and sooner or later they began acting like they are God Himself, not communicating with the common folks, forgetting where they came from, negatively talking about folks behind closed doors, using people for their own agendas, etc. Any time someone has to boast/prove themselves to look good with quoting scriptures each time they approach you, that person has other bad agendas he/she is hiding. We don't have to prove Jesus lives in us because it will show on its own. God will give us the words to say if He's ordering our footsteps. *Woe unto the shepherd who scatters My sheep.* It was just a matter of time before the above guy or the above preacher falls.

They gave my position to this guy and God didn't like the way and reason they did it, especially not based on job performance but politics. God knew it wasn't fair to me. Hidden actions for false agendas always surface, exposing reality. Abraham knew that he and Isaac were going to come down from that mountain simply because of God's earlier promise for Isaac. That was the same way I felt about the guy who replaced me because God gave me that position and He would certainly protect me. That's the reason I knew he wouldn't last in that position.

C: BROKEN HEART

Then I fell in love with this beautiful white girl from Iowa who loved me as much as I loved her. She was an analyst with the company and really didn't care about the color of my skin. This relationship didn't seem to bother anyone other than the guy who had taken my place. I really believe he would've accepted us if I wasn't the one who was beginning to expose his obvious wrongdoings. He knew the only way to get back at me was to destroy my relationship because he knew how strongly I felt about her. We dated for a long time, then we decided to move in together at my apartment. This taught me tremendous lessons about all different personalities because the same personality has the same behaviors. Our only problem was keeping our relationship secret from her parents who lived in Iowa. Her parents were against interracial relationships, especially their only daughter and worse, her living with a black man. Somehow my replacement found out about her parents' feelings, got access to her personnel files, got her parents' phone number, called them, and told them about us. Her parents went crazy and ordered her to return to Iowa immediately or they would have nothing else to do with her. We were devastated and she wanted to ignore her parents' request and remain with me. I didn't want to be the reason she lost her parents, so I decided we'd split up. She finally agreed but that was one of the worst hurts I'd ever felt because I really loved her.

A little later, my replacement's hidden problems surfaced and he could find no explanation but admission. The president got upset with the vice president for hiring him and not keeping up with all of his illegal activities. The president fired my replacement and had to ask me to take that position to clean up the mess that had been created. The woman that I loved moved back to Iowa and I saw her one last time about a year later. Does God deny relationships because of the color of our skins? I don't think so because we all were made in His own image, He knew us before we knew ourselves. He looks at our hearts/spirits instead of our outside appearances, and He is no respecter of man nor does He judge. I knew I had gotten my divorce and the relationship wasn't wrong, but the moving in together and sex were wrong in God's eyes. I didn't dislike her parents because of their beliefs, but because they "judged" me by the color of my skin. They didn't even know anything about my character or me, yet made a color judgment toward me due to a generational curse passed down to them. What if Jesus would've judged all of those unlike Him and refused to accept them? Although I was hurt, I let go because of all the confusion and Satan is the author of confusion.

Even in my mess, God revealed the details of the war I was fighting with my replacement. If we would've allowed God into our relationship letting Him order our footsteps, it may or may not have lasted. That would've depended on God's future plans for both of us. All things with God happen for reasons of His purpose and it's His will and not ours, His time and not ours, and His ways and not ours. Nothing gets in the way of God's plan and if it's meant to happen, it will; and if it's not meant to happen, it won't. God will allow things to happen to us because He probably has someone down the road to place in our paths going through the same thing He brought us out of. Even though sometimes the hurt is truly devastating to us, we need to praise Him because if it wasn't meant to be, the longer hurt is worse. God just shortens the levels of our suffering. How can we truly know what's best for us if we don't know our own future, not mentioning others? That's why we should praise Him in both good and bad. He will also make our enemies our footstools as He did with my replacement. Lots of things we have to go through just so there won't be any doubt as to who brought us out. Lots of our suffering when we go through things is self-inflicted because of our non-patience, non-belief, and non-trust that God will take away all of our pain. We ask the question, why the separation when we truly love another? It is simply because at that point, we feel the hurt will last forever. Sometimes when things don't go our way, we get upset with God, yet never do we look at whether our sins caused things to turn.

D: NEW MANAGEMENT

After I accepted taking back over my old position, the owner fired the president and brought in another president whom the old president was using as a consultant. This new president was snitching on the old president to the owner just to get the job. All the new president did was join in with my same old vice president and develop a new clique. Again, I put back together my kind of supervisors and store employees. I developed all my own control forms, and everything I needed to turn the company operations back around where I had them before. It took a little while to get there, but again, we ran some of the best numbers the company had ever seen. We received awards, bonuses, and special recognitions for all of our efforts during the years. I had gained so much respect that when we would have meetings, the employees would talk when other speakers would speak, but would be very quiet and listen when I was up speaking. When I spoke, I got down to their levels because I wanted them to understand totally what I was saying. When the meetings were over, I would always have almost all of the people who attended waiting to talk to me. Sometimes it would take longer than the meetings themselves when I would get finished talking to all of those who waited. I felt it was my obligation for them to know each one meant as much as the next to me. I never understood why it was so easy to draw so many different people to me. This also taught me to acknowledge different personalities and how to deal with each one of them separately. I learned you cannot treat all personalities the same and that extends to any part of life.

Everything was going great until a supervisor and myself began to question our marketing director's personal financial obligations vs. his high-class lifestyle. The numbers didn't add up so we started our own personal investigation knowing that no one would believe us unless we proved it. It took us a little time but we finally busted him cashing company checks, holding onto donated money for personal gain, etc. He went to prison. This move shocked the whole company and worse, the clique had lost a major link. This guy had thought he was better than anyone else and would always brag about himself, his college degree, his better material things, etc., trying to place himself above all others. He was one of the members of this clique and was also someone, again, my vice president brought over from the same company he came from. Birds of a feather flock together. It was also rumored that this marketing director did the same illegal things at their old company, yet just didn't get caught and my vice president knew of his dealings. This guy thought he had everybody fooled, he just didn't count on me not being fooled.

When people do us wrong because of their own ignorance or self-motivation, don't worry, especially if we're doing nothing wrong. Always remember that God is watching the whole thing and if we continue doing the right thing, God will move in. We don't have to do anything except wait on God. He will also send those who do us wrong back in front of us when they fall, and they will fall. It may take a day, week, month, or years, but they will fall, count on it. This is a good example showing a house divided cannot stand and when you've done all that you can do, just stand. If we're trying to always do the right thing, good will always come back to us. God will use the less of the lesser for His purpose even if we're not worth anything in the eyes of man. Even though others won't teach us because of jealousy or other motives, God will supply everything we need if we only ask and that includes knowledge. I was only a high school graduate with no college, so why would they want to listen or draw close to me? It wasn't me at all, they saw the Jesus in me from the seed planted long ago even though I didn't acknowledge that's what it was. Satan wasn't bothering me that much because I wasn't spending much time with him anymore. When Satan feels he's beginning to lose us, he throws all sorts of things at us trying to get us back on track with him. He gives us enough material rope, making us think it's long enough, just for us to hang ourselves. Bragging and boasting on material things are making those things our gods when there's nothing we need to put before our Almighty God. We don't understand that when we die, we can't take all of the money or material things with us either to heaven or hell. I would rather put God first in all and go to heaven rather than put material things before Him and go to hell. He said he would have no other god before Him! If we worship material things to the fullest because we don't want to lose them, we announce them as our gods.

E: NEW OWNERSHIP

The stolen losses and the mistrust the owner had were too much to hold the company together. The owner and his wife wanted out and sold the company. The clique thought I was a “nobody” and thought the best position I would get with the new company was store manager and they would still run the company. When all was said and done, all of them were out of a job and the new company hired my employees and me to operate the stores as one zone. The clique was shocked and utterly surprised. It took a few months before the final paperwork went through and the clique tried to make my life hell because they knew I would lead what they had failed to lead. They would be verbally sarcastic, conduct private meetings without me, hardly talk to me, etc., all of the negative behaviors because of their jealousy. They couldn’t blame me because I didn’t have anything to do with the selections, yet they tried to take their personal disappointments out on me. Never did any of them recall or remember what they had done to me or how they hurt me. My happiness wasn’t for bragging rights, but because God had stepped in letting them know they could not hurt people for their own satisfactions and greed. By them doing me wrong, my face was the last one they had to see, with me being on top and them going out the door. Seems like God will put us back in front of those whom we have done wrong after we have fallen. We have to be very careful how we treat people because what we sow, so shall we reap. We may hide our bad from man, but we can’t hide anything from God. They didn’t realize God had other plans for me and Satan had them totally deceived. Jesus picked a plain ol’ fisherman for His first disciple, so why not plain ol' me? We have to stop thinking we're not as good because everything we lack, God will supply. Try Him and dare Him to do what He promised! We need to rely on and put our faith in God and not in man because man will let us down, but God will lift us up.

CHAPTER FOUR

Second Marriage

A: IN LOVE AT SATAN'S DEN

I was living in this very nice apartment and had met a couple that became best friends of mine. Although I wasn't drinking as much during the week, we would always find time on weekends to get drunk. I would throw parties at home, go over to my relatives' homes, go to military clubs with my friends, or whatever ongoing function to have fun, we thought, and drinks. There was no thought of my completely walking with God, let alone going to church. I felt like I was advancing on my own and my life was getting better and better. During my leisure time I would write poetry but it always seemed there was something else missing in my life. I would have short relationships with different women and became very jealous of my male friend having only one woman. They seemed like the perfect couple and I only wished that one woman would love me as much as she seemed to have loved my best friend. Later they moved out of the apartment complex into a beautiful house. I would go to visit and again became very jealous of their home and relationship. I prayed that one day I would find that special woman and have a nice home as my best friend had. They weren't married at that time, but just living together. They finally decided to get married and I was asked to stand in their wedding, which made me more envious of them. They had the ceremony at a military chapel and their reception was at this club they frequented a lot. After the ceremony, we went to the club where all of us got very drunk. Everybody in the club seemed to be drinking, dancing, singing, and everything we thought to be having fun. Suddenly, I turned to my right, saw this light-skinned, beautiful, long black-haired, nicely dressed woman sitting with another woman and talking to this man who was also sitting at the table. A song that I liked came on, not knowing if she was with the guy, and went over and asked her to dance. She accepted and when the song was over, I went and sat with her the rest of the evening. I also told her that night that I was going to marry her.

After the reception was over, she went home with me and stayed the night. Many times, even while God is blessing us, we're not satisfied, yet wanting more. Why do we get envious of others who have a little more than we have? If God wanted us to have more, He would have given us more. Instead of thanking God for what He has blessed us with, we cause ourselves to wonder if God loves the others more. We forget that we are not even trying to walk with God yet we want Him to give us more and better blessings. Even when we are not hurting for anything, we still get jealous of others. We want it both ways and even continuing in our mess, we have the nerve to ask God for better blessings. Many times we judge others' relationships from the surface not knowing of the hell raised behind their closed doors. Many times the ones we're jealous of are still serving Satan and we're not realizing that the very things we are jealous of are not going to last.

That's exactly what happened to my best friends after a few years. Now, was it worth all of the hurt I put upon myself by being jealous of them? Lots of times we ask God to bless us with things like others and we get just what we ask for, including the unseen bad. We must be careful of what we ask for making sure we define our desires to God. Satan wants us as much as God does and he will set up the stage that appeals to our every desire, just as we like it. If we are not walking with God, we won't be able to distinguish a difference, thus being deceived by Satan. We were definitely in Satan's den when we were in that club because there was nothing of God there. Satan had total control over everything that happened that night from beginning to ending. Did Satan send her to me or was she a gift from God? Many times when we think God is sending us something or someone, we're being set up by Satan. We are so deceived by Satan that we won't know the difference until it's too late.

B: DREAMS DO COME TRUE

When I finally went to her apartment, I found out that she had birthed a six-month old girl, a seven-year-old boy, and a ten-year-old girl. This bothered my family more than it did me because I felt if I wanted her, the kids went with the package. There is no way you can accept the mother and not the kids. We went on little trips to parks, carnivals, etc., and enjoyed each other very much. After a while of getting, we thought, to know each other very well, we decided to move in together. At that time I had gotten my credit in shape and decided that instead of paying for an apartment big enough for all of us, I would try to buy a house. She had a good job and so did I, so we could afford the payments of a house.

One Sunday we went looking with a realtor and fell in love with this nice two-story house. I submitted all of the paperwork and about a month later, the realtor called and I was approved for the house. I couldn't believe I could be blessed with a home like I saw and had prayed about when I was just a kid. We took the furniture we both had accumulated in our apartments and moved into the house. All we didn't have, we used my credit cards and purchased the rest. We painted and decorated it exactly how both of us had dreamed our home would look. The home was in a very nice neighborhood of middle- to upper-class with mostly white residents. The schools were great and everything around was how I always dreamed of living. My company was selling some extra cars and I bought one for my woman, giving both of us separate transportation. All of this was definitely a dream come true. We also had gotten each other fine jewelry over the years. I was especially fond of my fourteen-karat gold nugget ring with a horseshoe on top, my Gucci diamond watch, and my fourteen-karat gold bracelet. We even turned our two-car garage into an office, a den, a utility room, and a tool room.

God gives us the desires of our hearts but where we fall short is not giving Him the praise. Earlier in life when I was very young, I prayed for a family, nice car, big house, and a good job where I could wear a tie to work. God gave all of that to me, mostly at one time and even with me not completely serving Him. Many times God gives us the basics to see how we handle them, then gradually gives us the others to complete our dreams. God took my magazine desires from childhood and made them a reality. God wants us to have the very best in life, but we, not Him, set ourselves up to lose everything by forgetting about Him after we're blessed. We get impatient and want all of it at one time as though God is moving too slowly. That's where we get ourselves in trouble because "we" try to do it and not wait on God. Satan is hanging around telling us God has started it, now we can finish it and we don't need God's help anymore. We start putting our material blessings before God and He said we would put nothing before Him. We had crosses, religious pictures, etc., in our home thinking those were sufficiently praising and honoring Him. We make that mistake all of the time, not understanding God wants a personal relationship with Him and not an ornament hanging on a wall. He wants our hearts to represent Him and not something manmade. This also proves that God is not a respecter of man, that what He does for others, He'll do for us. He also placed us in a neighborhood I used to be envious of while growing up in my hometown. Back in those days, the only ones living in those areas were the whites and the only times we went into those neighborhoods was to work.

C: SATAN'S CEREMONY

Each weekend we would get with close friends and take the families to all kinds of places. The one thing we never left was our drinks and music because getting drunk and listening to the blues was a requirement. Many times we should've been dead from a wreck or thrown in jail, but we always made it to and from all of our destinations. When we didn't go out of town on weekends, we would throw house parties inviting friends and relatives. We would get drunk, listen to loud music, play dominoes, dance, and sing until the early hours of the morning. Instead of praising God the next day, we'd start all over again. The only thing I was unhappy with was when the kids' father would come over to pick them up and after a couple of days, bring them back. It seemed to me he was taking them away from me even though they would call both of us Dad. The main bother was the fact that they had his blood and not mine, which caused me to somehow feel threatened by that. I wanted the kids all to myself and didn't understand why I had to share them when it was me they called for late at night. With everything seeming to be going so well, we decided to get married and make our relationship legal. We decided to have the ceremony and reception in the back yard of our home and have my best friend with his wife stand as best man.

Things didn't go as planned on our wedding day. I didn't have the right kind of socks, my wife's best friend flirted with me, I had already begun to drink liquor, I was being married by a preacher who was living with my little cousin, the video camera was not focusing right, and my baby daughter wanted her mother to pick her up during the vows. Among these and many other problems that happened, we continued to go ahead with Satan ignoring God's signs. As soon as the preacher pronounced us man and wife, a storm came, causing us to put everything inside of the house to have the reception. All of the nice set-up and decorating we did in the backyard was useless. That didn't stop us from partying and opening our gifts until the early morning hours.

The next morning the house inside and outside was horrible and it took us all day to clean it up. Satan is so convincing and had us so deceived, we believed everything was so wonderful. He puts people and things in our lives to promote his false happiness. As long as we are having fun today, we don't think of tomorrow. That's fine to practice if you're serving God, but disaster if you're serving Satan. Satan had us completely bound because he knew we only wanted to have fun and keep the blessings we had. He had us thinking we had the best of both worlds even when we would take those trips with our friends on weekends. Satan also knew that my stepkids were very special to me and that we were building a close relationship, so he decided to remind me I was not their blood father. He knew if he convinced me to make an issue of that, I would create confusion in the household, putting strife between the blood father and me. He also had me suspect my wife of still having feelings for the father. It never occurred to me that the person that's there all of the time caring for them would be the one most remembered in their older ages. Even up to this writing, I am still very close and Dad to all of those kids. Of course, Satan didn't want me to think that way at the time. We always say and think that God joins together all marriages, but look at our circumstances before, during, and after our ceremony. Was any of it of God and was He in our presence? He said when two or more come in His name, He'll be in the midst and there was none who came in His name. What about the preacher who was living with and intimate with my cousin without being married, is that of God? Was he ordained to marry us before he cleaned up his act? Does

God send or ordain people to promote or join together sin, especially when all know it's sin? What about all of the confusion before the vows, is God the author of confusion? What about the storm that immediately came after we became married, who controls the weather? Even with all of the small signs and the large storm sign, we still refused to listen.

When God plans something, everything is in order. We need to stop figuring that God ordained all marriages until we analyze the whole situations before and after the vows. Then we must ask ourselves if God was part of it or not. Instead of waiting on God to give us our companion, we take matters into our own hands and suffer from our decision wondering why it doesn't work. There are always signs warning us to beware of making mistakes, yet we choose to ignore them, especially when the outcome isn't what we want. All of the signs we encountered should've made us reconsider but we didn't. Instead of what God has joined together, shouldn't we say, what man has joined together? Truly answering the question will answer our marriage future.

D: DOWNWARD SPIRAL OF FINANCES

As the kids grew up, each year we tried to "keep up with the Joneses" losing control of all our financial obligations. We began living from week to week, yet still had to keep the parties going. Each Christmas we had to give our kids everything they had asked for and I would sell my vacation each year to pay for our total Christmas. I would put thousands of lights both inside and outside of our house just to keep up with the neighbors and make my kids happy. We had charged up all of our credit cards where they were in the over-limit status. One year we were going out of town to visit our closest friends for Christmas and the week before leaving, we wrote checks for all of the kids' gifts. The day of leaving I went into the office to get the president to sign my vacation pay request, get the check cut, then go and deposit it into the bank so the checks wouldn't bounce. When I got there, the president had left town for the holidays and there was nobody in the office authorized to sign my request. I had to get the money into the bank that day because the banks were closed the following day. I was frantic because I didn't know what to do and I had about $1,500 worth of checks to hit the bank that night or the following business day.

I got back home, talked to my wife, decided there wasn't anything else I could do but hope they didn't hit until the evening after the holidays, then decided to continue with our plans. I left a message with the only management person in the office to tell the comptroller my problem if and when he returned to the office. We were on our way and it was about an hour before all banks would close and even though I was sipping on liquor, I was still stressed. As soon as I accepted to face the consequences when the checks bounced which was now about thirty minutes before the banks closed, my cell phone rang. It was the guy I left a message with telling me the comptroller had just come in and agreed to cut the check even without the president's signature. He also told me that he would try to get to the bank before it closed and deposit the check for me. About forty minutes later, he called and told me to go ahead and enjoy myself because he made it to the bank on time. I just shouted and instead of me thanking God, I just made me a stronger drink.

About halfway to our destination and after I had gotten halfway drunk, the police pulled us over twice for speeding. I only received two speeding tickets even though each officer knew I was drunk, but the second officer made me turn over the driving to my wife. When we got there in the snow, my car window had to be broken because we had locked the keys inside the car with the engine still running. We put plastic over the window, went inside, partied that night, and all of the other days/nights we were there. When we were about to go home after a few days, I couldn't start the car because of the heavier oil I had put in at home. Finally after the weather warmed up, the car started and we had to drive home in the cold because of the broken window, but had no other problems.

Most times we place all of our trust in man instead of God and believe there is a guarantee with man. Writing those checks before I got the vacation check deposited was depending on man. But why not when I was still serving

Satan with the parties and getting drunk? Each time I would spend extra money on Christmas lights or put more on the credit cards knowing our funds were already limited, I'd allow Satan to convince me that some way I'd get the money to pay those bills. Satan knows we won't get the money and have to borrow from Peter to pay Paul until we get seriously in trouble. He always deceives us into thinking that somehow we're going to "luck up" on some mysterious money to catch the bills up. Of course, that's a mirage and we continue to spend our paycheck before it's even printed. It gets to the point where we pay the most critical bills and lie to the creditors about the ones we can't pay. We are always given the choice before we get ourselves in trouble; God reminds us of that option yet most if not all times we choose the wrong one. Even in my mess with the checks, God loved me enough to come to my rescue like He did with Abraham. Even with my drunkenness, he sent me a "ram in the bush." We serve an "on time" God. Looks like when we totally give up, that's when God comes through. God knew if that amount of checks had bounced, I would've gotten in serious trouble with the law, which would've interrupted His plan for me. When those two officers stopped me for speeding, my drunkenness should've sent me to jail ruining my family's entire Christmas weekend, not even counting all of the compounded financial sufferings. God loved me enough to make those cops allow us to continue our trip even driving with an obvious drunk until my wife was told to take over.

Even with the broken window and car not starting, God warmed up the oil enough so we could get back home. It seems like God overruled Satan as He did with telling Satan that he could try Job, but he could not kill him.

E: WIFE'S FRIENDS

Suddenly, my wife became more interested in her friends and going to clubs than her family. She allowed one of her friends to cause her to lose her good job, which threw an additional financial burden on us. It had gotten so bad that there were charges of gas and beer on our gas card that didn't match up with our receipt copies. Plus there were two or three gas fill-ups during weeks and I knew she wasn't driving that much, yet filling up her friends' cars. My investigation showed that she was supplying all of her friends' needs when they would go out, playing "Mrs. Big Shot." She would always get mad and defend them when I would try to discuss the problems I was having with them and of course, her being used. This seemed to make her go out with them more and push us further apart. There was lots of disrespect toward the family with her coming in the early morning hours when they'd go to a club, have male/female friends congregate in our upstairs bedroom when I'd come home from work, maybe cook then leave to go play cards many times a week, etc. When we'd go to visit our relatives, she'd rush to leave so she could go out with her friends. Most all of her friends she hung around with were single women and many of them didn't have kids. My wife wanted to be single and married at the same time. Almost everywhere we went together, we had an argument about something, unlike before with us agreeing on almost everything. Our marriage was slowly deteriorating and there seemed to be nothing we could say or do to stop it. We certainly didn't seek religious counseling. There was no doubt that her single friends were coaching her in her actions toward our kids and me. She didn't want to have any more kids, yet she agreed she would have a child with our blood. Although I loved my stepchildren with all of my heart, I was jealous that she had given her previous men their own child and not me. I asked God to send me a boy through the woman that I married and loved. I described him from head to foot including his skin color to God in prayer.

Nine months later, my wife gave birth to a healthy baby boy, which still didn't change anything in our relationship. That baby was identical to the one I had described in my prayer without deviation. Later, those same friends evaporated like water in hot sun, especially in my wife's time of need. Close friends become jealous especially when you have what they don't and have always wanted. If you're on a higher level than them, they will do all they can to bring you back down to their level. As long as they can use you for their benefit, they'll hang around, but when you can't provide, they'll drop you to find another weak one. How can a single friend counsel a married person, especially if they haven't been married before? How can an ungodly person tell you about God? Single friends will talk negative about your other half simply because of jealousy or trying themselves to take your other half for themselves. The first thing they will tell you is, "Girl/Man, I wouldn't put up with all of that, I'd leave that alone." As soon as you take their advice and leave, they'll be the first ones trying to move in on where you left. Friends with their own agendas don't care about your family because their only obligations is themselves. My wife had everything that a thirty-year-old woman with her background could ever dream of yet she allowed her friends to cause a void. When you're falling on hard times or have allowed yourself to be used up, those same so-called close friends will leave you standing by yourself. All they will do is find some other weak soul to use. I don't know why this surprises us because even Jesus' disciples left Him after He was arrested. Even Peter denied Jesus three times when he claimed never to leave Him. Even Judas betrayed Jesus for greed. God answered my prayer and gave me the exact son I had described to Him, identical. God knew my heart and all of the things I was going through. Even with all my faults, He heard my prayer. When we're serving Satan, there will always be confusion, arguments, mistrust, weakness, etc., because by keeping us that way, we'll make bad decisions. God will stick with us closer than a brother.

F: UNKNOWN SURPRISES

Around 2 a.m. one morning while in a deep sleep, the phone started ringing and it was something about that ring just made me not want to answer. I allowed it to ring a long time before deciding to pick it up. It was my stepbrother in Houston telling me that my mother had just died in her sleep. I immediately became sad, confused, mad, shocked, and all different emotions tied into one. After getting my kids up, telling them their grandmother had died, and getting our clothes together, we went to the car to leave. My wife wasn't at home because she had gone out with her friends. As soon as we were about to back out of the driveway, my wife, who had just come from a club, drove up, asking where were we going. After I told her that my mother had died, she started screaming with tears because she and my mother were very close. She immediately went into the house, called the kids' dad to keep them, packed some clothes, and left with us. She stayed by my side from that moment until we buried my mother.

After the funeral, she and the kids drove back home while I went to Houston for a few days to make sure my stepfather was going to be fine. It was around my wife's birthday and I had no idea until I got back home that she and her friends had a party in our house the same evening she got back home from the funeral. I had thought maybe my mother's death would bring us closer together, especially when she was partying when my mother died, but it didn't. I was also bringing my handicapped brother back to live with us because my stepfather was too old to handle him. My mom had kept him at home all of his life and cared for him. All of my relatives and my wife had assured me during the funeral not to worry because they would help me with him. I was working twelve-hour days and had no idea about schools, financials, medicines, or anything concerning the welfare of a handicapped person. My wife had agreed she would care for him while I was at work because she wasn't working and she had the time.

Well, that only lasted for a few days and she told me that she just couldn't handle it any longer. One of the major problems was she couldn't party with her friends all day while I was at work anymore. I didn't know what to do, so I looked in the phone book, found this adult daycare, and called them. They enrolled him the very next day, which worked out for me in dropping him off in the mornings and picking him up before 8 p.m. each evening. The schedule was only Monday through Friday but I could handle him myself on weekends because I was off most all of them. The weekends I worked, I was just on call and if I got a call, I took him with me. The evenings I had to work late because of meetings, etc., my little cousin would pick him up and keep him until I got off. Our marriage got worse and I kept finding books on apartments under our mattress, so I knew it was just a matter of time before it was over.

Finally she decided she was moving out and told me what she was going to take out of the house. I agreed and one night she and her friends drove up in a u-haul, loaded all of her stuff, and drove off. We had also agreed that I would take custody of our new baby boy who was two years of age at that time. I had no idea how I would take care of him, my brother, and still work my long hours, but I had no other choice. I put my baby boy in daycare and my brother was already going to his adult daycare, which helped me because I could drop them and pick them up basically around the same time. It was very hard but somehow I got the strength to do it. I was shocked when I heard from my neighbor that my wife and her friends had come back the following day trying to get back into the house and couldn't. After she left, I was so tired but I gained the strength to change the locks. I'm not sure if my brother's presence broke the last straw in our marriage, but he had no one else but me and I wasn't going to turn my back on him.

When Satan has a hold on us, it seems like we trade even the dearest things to us for a life with him. We are so deceived into thinking that we are the center and everything around us is supposed to stand still. Just when we don't expect anything to happen, Satan's business as usual, we encounter a personal shockwave. Life assumes it would make us snap, but for most of us, it only lasts a little while, even when it's meant to get our attention. We all need to be saved because we don't know when it's our time to leave here. Sometimes we fool ourselves thinking that we can save people from the hands of Satan and send them to heaven. All we can do is tell them the Word and try to get them to establish a personal relationship with Jesus, that's our only job. Once we give them the word, we've planted or watered a seed because His Word doesn't come back void. He is the only One who has the ultimate power to change and heal. It is definitely harder if we are not living right ourselves. Satan doesn't care if we don't like the way he's guiding his followers because he wants them as far away from God's children as possible. He'll make sure their entertainment is readily available just to keep them on his side. Always be careful, listen well, and don't expect anything when we're at our worst and people promise us they'll be there for us. Most times those are only words and the moment we really need them, there's always an excuse. This happens with relatives, close friends, spouses, or anyone else who want to make themselves look good in front of others. That gives them a sense of importance at our sorrow's expense. If they only agree to help when they're in front of an audience, beware because their guarantee isn't worth anything. God is the only One who won't leave or forsake us and unlike us, He keeps His promises. Even when we're confused and feel like we can't go on, if we ask, God will give us the strength to overcome anything.

I felt like I was out there alone with my son and brother, then God opened doors even without me asking. God answers prayers even before we ask. God also knew my wife and friends were going to return the next day probably to take the rest of the things out of the house, so that's why He gave me the strength to change the locks the night before when I didn't feel like it. There is no doubt she would've cleaned me out like my first marriage but God protected me. Everything is showing me that my marriage had no chance to succeed because from the beginning until the end, God was not included. Even though He showed us His grace many times, we chose not to acknowledge or praise Him because our bad overruled our good.

G: SINGLE PARENT OBSTACLES AND SO-CALLED STEPS

I found myself into the role of a single parent of a two-year-old son and a forty-year-old brother working twelve hours a day. It was like being a parent to my brother because of his limits toward doing for himself and his jealousy when I took more time with my son than him. Even in the early morning hours when I had to go to an emergency on my job, I had to wake both of them up and take them with me. Most times they would only get a couple of hours of sleep before waking back up after we returned home. It was hard on all of us, especially them. So many times I'd be so tired when I finally went to bed, I couldn't fall to sleep.

Among all of this, one day I received a call that my stepfather had died. I also found out that not long after my mom had died, his children had admitted him into a nursing home and had sold and taken everything in my parents' house. Probably sixty percent of the nice things were purchased by me for them, yet my brother and I didn't get anything, not even the family pictures. My mom had lots of expensive jewelry which I would've loved to have for her granddaughters. There was no need to try to fight for any because it was all gone the day I found out about my stepfather's death.

A few weeks later, a stepbrother called and told me, after we all agreed to sell the house, that my brother and I would get fifty percent and all of them would split the other fifty percent. He was saying that we would get our mother's half and they would get their father's half. It was more of them than us and I guess they figured that each of their shares would be much less than ours. Then they went back on their agreement knowing what the law said and equally divided the proceeds between all of the children. I thought they would divide it by the first agreement since they took all of the house items, which would've been only fair, but I didn't fight it. To this day, I believe they found a handwritten will leaving everything to my brother and me because my stepfather always told me not to worry because we would "always have a roof over our head." I believe they found and destroyed it right after my mom had died when they went through everything in their house. I suspect this because when my stepfather died, they tried to use one of my mom's insurance policies I didn't find when she died to help bury my stepfather. The funeral director denied using it and told my cousin to call and tell me what happened. How low can you go? Even with the denial, they still didn't send the policy to me.

During these times, I began to seek God more and had cut down on my drinking and partying a lot. I didn't have time for it at all during the week, yet some weekends and special holidays, I still got drunk. During this time, I know I prayed a lot not knowing if God would hear my prayers because of my sins. As time went by, things with my brother started falling apart. I'm not sure if it was because of him finally missing my mom or not. He couldn't express himself vocally because he'd never been able to talk. He would refuse to let me help him up and down the in-house stairs. Several times he fell having to go to the hospital. He would eat and have bowel movements on himself and all over the house, which would make me extremely mad. I'm ashamed to say, but a few times I would be so tired and upset, it got physical and afterwards, I would feel so bad. He couldn't help himself or he would just do it to express hurt he felt for my mom's death.

When we would go for a drive and I'd park to run into a store, he would get out of the car and walk. It would stress me out because I had to find him before he hurt himself and wouldn't know where he had walked. He would get mad at my son, make cursing gestures, and had to be restrained because of his extreme anger. He was on daily medication for his seizures, yet I had to always be alert because he would still have them consistently. Even after long hours at work, I would still have to fix dinner every night because he couldn't take his medication without eating before. Before my brother got into the daycare, I would have to wake up early in the morning, drop off my son at his daycare, drive about twenty miles on the other side of town, drop off my brother at my aunt's, then work twelve hours, and take the same route back home each evening. On top of that, I had to still fix dinner so they could eat. This lasted for a good while, but that was the only thing I could do, I had no choice. I had placed my brother's name on the list at a home to keep him all of the time, but they told me it would probably take years before they would have an opening. Each home I inquired about told me the same thing and the thought of me doing this for years and years scared me, but what could I do but accept it?

I incurred this for about two and a half years, which took a real toll on me. The straw that broke the camel's back was one morning before we left on our route, my brother fell down the stairs cutting himself over the eyes. I knew the cut needed stitches, so I immediately got my son and rushed him to the hospital. When I got back home I cried out to God to help me because I just couldn't take anymore. I knew I was at my breaking point. Shortly after crying out, the phone rang and it was this home center telling me another family canceled their loved one's bed and asking if I wanted it. I didn't hesitate in telling them that I wanted it and that I would go over to sign the papers the next day. The employee told me if I wanted it, I needed to go right over or they'd assign it to someone else.

I called my job, took the day off, and we went over to the home. They showed me around and I loved it. When we sat down to complete the paperwork, the employee asked me if I still wanted the room because the family whose room we were taking called back changing their minds. After answering her we did, she told me it was ours but by law, she had to ask. Three days later, I took my brother to the home and left him, but I couldn't explain the guilt I felt. I was thinking that my mom had kept him all of those years and I couldn't even make it three years. The thing that eased my mind was visiting my brother one day and seeing him love his surroundings not wanting to leave. Then I was satisfied and felt no guilt realizing that God made that happen. The home was equipped with doctors, nurses, scheduled meals. He had his own room, twenty-four-hour monitoring, etc., everything needed for my brother's well being. It is so funny how people change when there is death inheritance involved. All of us are so close when people are alive, but as soon as they're not, money becomes the strongest dividers. Money is the root of all evil making us wonder what happened to the close relationships we previously had. Of course, Judas betrayed and changed on Jesus for money, so why would we expect anything less from our relations? If we think our closest relatives, including our brothers and sisters, won't change on us, just let someone close to both of us die. It will certainly expose the lie we were living when we were faking this close-knit relation. Also, other people and relatives who hadn't been close to us or even given us the time or day, will get so close to us when someone dies because they think we're coming into some type of inheritance. Once they see we're not going to get the amount they thought we were going to get, watch them scatter. These reactions are not about God, instead they're about fleshly greed. We need to ask God to stop us from fighting over someone else's stuff, even if we have a share, and ask Him to fight that battle for us. Not only will He take care of you, He'll expose what your enemy tries to do to you.

Not long after they sold all of my parents' household things, the stepbrother who had planned it all had a serious illness. We can't do God's people wrong and expect to get away with it. God knew of the manipulation, greed, sneakiness, unfairness, etc., these once "supposed to have been" step-relatives of mine had planned, even from their beginning. With all of the things I had to learn and went through with my brother, God knew He had to give me strength to deal with it. Although I wasn't serving God as fully as I should've been, I still looked up to Heaven from which came my strength. My strength did come from the Lord because I would've gone totally insane if I would have depended on others or myself. When I was going through all of this with my brother, God was just waiting on me to call on Him instead of Satan, even when He already had it worked out. *Come to me all ye who labor with a heavy laden and I'll give you rest.*

Satan used my weaknesses to strike back at my brother's illness, even physically. Satan would've had me getting drunk every day trying to cover up my problems, but when I asked God for help, He allowed me to go through some more, but He knew my limit. Satan can only do what God allows and he doesn't know our limits, only God.

The last morning my brother fell down the stairs and I cried out to God, He was the One who made the other family cancel their relative's bed, opening a door for me. What are the chances of that happening when the place had others on their list who had registered before me that should've been called? God heard my cry and knew I was at my limit.

H: BROKEN DREAMS

My son and I lived in my dream home until I just couldn't afford to make the payments any longer. I had child support, bankruptcy payments, and high taxes being taken out of my paycheck each week leaving me barely enough to live on. The monthly checks for my brother's disability had transferred to the home he was living in and I couldn't count on that anymore. I used to sit in the living room, look at the blessings that God had given me, and thank Him knowing that I was going to be forced to give my home up. Even before I got into this shape, my son and I went looking for a new vehicle because my old car started giving me problems. My credit wasn't that good but I decided to seek anyway. Every car lot we went to and found the vehicle I wanted, something would always come up where I couldn't get it. I prayed to God about it but thought after a long time looking and being denied, He didn't want us to have one. Also I had filed for bankruptcy and had to have a judge sign an approval for me to buy a vehicle. God made that happen.

One weekend we decided to take a ride and look one more time at vehicles even knowing our negative chances. The place was closed and again I thought God didn't want us to have one. The next day something told me to go back out there and when we got there, we saw a dream SUV, did the paperwork on it, and left thinking there was no way we were going to get that new vehicle, especially when we were denied the used ones.

The next morning, I received a call from the place telling me I was approved and I could come that same evening to pick my dream car up. When driving it home, all I could do was praise and thank God. All of the other vehicles had 30,000-plus mileage, yet this one only had three miles.

It had gotten to the time we had to be out of my dream home and every place we wanted to rent, there wasn't enough time or we couldn't afford it. A few days before we had to be out, I found a house, which was my last option to rent and moved in. My son and I had no help packing and moving until the next day, which only were two more people, but we moved everything out. One thing we have to understand is when God wants us to move in order for His plan to be fulfilled, we are going to move one way or the other. If it's His will for us to stay, He'll provide the way through blessings. Sometimes God allows us to lose things that really mean a lot to us, just to turn our attention to Him. He places us in bad positions then brings us out just to get us to realize that the only One who could've done that was Him. God tests our patience to see if we trust Him enough and if you believe that He's able to do all things. When we feel it's the last minute when blessings come through for us, we don't realize that God had already been working on them on our behalf. He knows what our situations are and what we need, but sometimes we pout and try to rush God. We forget His time is not our time and His ways are not our ways. Why can't we just trust and believe in Him? God caused my sub-standard credit be good enough to approve the desire of my heart. There was no way other than God's will that I should've been approved for that new vehicle. He also wants and gives us the best instead of just settling for what we feel we can only get. We elected to rush, feel less of ourselves, have a "want it right now" attitude, allow Satan's salesman to overrule our belief in God, and many other emotional actions of our flesh. When God blesses us, it's normally the same time or right after we've given up. If it were left up to fleshly me, I would've taken the first high mileage vehicle and would've missed out because look what God had waiting for me. Wait on the Lord because He doesn't gives up on us like we give up on Him so quickly. When God puts His stamp of approval on something, man cannot disapprove it no matter what or how hard he/she tries, nor how bad our situation looks.

CHAPTER FIVE

Downhill Journey on Job

A: BIRTH PAST SURFACING

The company where I worked for eighteen years had finally sold. I never thought during those years about not having retirement when I left or what I would do if the company folded. It's a strange feeling when you've put in all of those years and have no kind of financial security afterwards. The new company gave me credit for my years only toward my vacation, but not tenure with the company. I couldn't blame the new company because that wouldn't have been fair to their long-term employees who put in the blood and sweat to gain all of their years. It was like I was starting all over again, but at least I was hired in as a zone manager and had a job with the new company. Many employees lost their jobs. The only problem with this was being the first and only black in this company to hold that position. The perception from all of the other "down-South mentality" zone managers was I had no business in the position, that I was a failure from the beginning, blacks don't belong in high positions, and they weren't going to provide any help to me. I went into the job with a "get him out" target painted on my back with their demeanor and behavior making it quite evident I didn't belong there.

With everything else in my life, now I had to deal with segregation. My first zone meeting was horrible because of my having to beg my ex-wife to keep my son while I was gone and the way I was treated during the meeting. At this meeting we sat at a large circular table facing each other with the COO asking us questions about our bad numbers in our zone. When it was my turn, all eyes were on this new black man who had no sense or business sitting at the table in their views. I gave my answers and during the breaks, the others would speak because of courtesy but none of them would stop to hold a conversation with me. I felt so alone because most of the time, I was by myself and couldn't wait until it was all over. The thing this taught me was to learn how their game was played, that I had to make my own name, and how to gain the determination that I was going to beat all of them in numbers. Thank God I had to learn on my own all those years at the previous company because that was something even they couldn't take away from me. I would need that experience and more to beat all of the odds that were against me being successful. Sometimes we find ourselves asking why things didn't go the way we expected them to go, especially in our older years. One thing we have to remember is that God knows our beginning to our ending and He has a purpose for each of our lives. God knew there was no retirement at the old company and He would've changed my employment if it was not planned out for His purpose. Sometimes He puts us in awkward positions like me being the only black because we need that experience in His future plans. He also prepares us previously for each encounter we have to go through before we even go through it. He knew I wouldn't have probably called on Him if there were other blacks in my position and sitting at that meeting table. He wanted all odds against me so I could overcome them and give Him all the praise. Unlike flesh judging each by the color of his/her skin, God looks at the spirit of the heart. I had to realize that God was my retirement.

We must remember when we are doing bad, there's always someone else who is doing worse than us. We must praise God in the bad the same as we do in the good. We must also acknowledge that God controls all and trust Him enough to know He knows what He is doing. When we are around ignorance, we must always remember that prejudices are all manmade. Greater is He that's in us, than he that's in the world need to be cemented into our memories.

B: BEATING THE ODDS

The first thing I had to do was put my inherited

supervisors who had old habits and didn't want to work for a black man in check. They were fighting me tooth and nail having a direct line to my boss when things didn't go their way. The problem I was having with my boss was he was allowing them to get away with it. I knew they were going to hang themselves if I gave them enough rope and they did. Their districts began to show the worst numbers in my zone and they didn't have legitimate answers for their losses. After so many losses, my boss had to give me the full control over them and cut off his communication with them. I started posting all of each supervisor's numbers on the conference room's wall so everyone could see each supervisor's numbers. Both of them were embarrassed because their fellow supervisors were seeing how bad they looked and how vain without merit their answers were. I knew everything going on in each store in each district, so they just couldn't give me any excuse. When they did, I embarrassed them in front of everybody to gain respect. They soon decided to do their jobs my way, come to me for help, and not try to hide problems from me. I had all of them to email all of the numbers I required to me every day and I would stay up late to analyze each one of them. I expected action on problems immediately, especially on employee names I had consistently associated with problems.

My previous years had taught me how to deal with different personalities because the same behavior always acted the same. I had another supervisor who was brought over with me from our old company and protected by my old president until this supervisor made him look bad. This guy would always con and play politics with the upper management, gaining their confidence. He also played that role with my boss with the new company, gaining his confidence also. He didn't fool me and he knew it, but it still didn't stop him from trying. At the end, I beat him at his own game and had him quitting instead of me firing him, which was better for the company. I refused to allow anyone or anything stand in my way that would keep me from looking good at the next corporate meeting. I had learned how to do my job and I was good at it. The other two I was having problems with ended up with one making it and the other one fired for stealing.

Satan has followers also and he places them in our paths to make it hard for us to reach our goals. They have hopes we turn to Satan with drunkenness, giving up, drugs, etc., because those behaviors show weakness. He tries to keep our minds so confused we don't have time to think about calling on God for help. All of the above supervisors who didn't want me there didn't know who I had watching over me. Sometimes it looked like they had the upper hand or were going to win, but I just hung on in there, did the right things, and waited for God to expose them. When you allow God to fix or expose a problem, not only is it fixed for now, it's fixed for life where you don't have to worry about that particular problem again. When we try to fix the problem ourselves, we mess it up so bad that the same problem comes back over and over. Always remember, Satan is the author of confusion and his people will confuse themselves so much and think they're indispensable that they'll choke on their own vomit with us just sitting back watching. That's what happened to the above guys and as soon as they thought they were on top of their game, the rug was pulled from under them, with them wondering what happened and why. Each one of us needs a Judas in our lives because we need to experience a betrayal from someone we trusted. That way we will recognize the next Judas coming from a long distance and can teach others the experience we've learned. No weapon formed against me shall prosper! When others fight against God's followers, they aren't fighting against them, but the God in them. They are also fighting against God's purposes and plans. How does anyone expect to win if they're battling against God? Or does Satan have them so confused, they don't even realize who their opponent is?

C: MEETINGS WITH GOD AND SATAN

The company scheduled many meetings in different cities and we were required to attend each of them. Many times we had to pay our own expenses up front, then be reimbursed by the company at a later date. I still had costly deductions coming out of my checks and really couldn't afford additional expenses along with my normal bills. I couldn't go to the company and claim my situation because I didn't want to look bad to my fellow zone managers who had money to spend or taking the chance of the company replacing me because I couldn't afford the expenses of the meetings. Satan threw many obstacles in my way wanting me to give up, stress out, get jealous of the others, or embarrass myself informing the company of my financial situation. This would've also been bad for the next black person coming up after me considered for a corporate type of promotion.

After every meeting, the company would pay for dinner and alcoholic drinks for all of us. We would eat and drink until the early mornings, always getting drunk. It seemed the drunker we got, the more fun we had with upper management because they would also be drunk. Satan had all of us serving him. These consistent meetings would also keep me angry and at odds with my ex-wife because she had to keep my son during my absences, which took her away from her outings. She would have me so bitter at times I would carry that angry behavior to the meetings wondering if she was mistreating our son because of me. Each meeting had gotten better and better with my good numbers and presentations. Initially they would test me by asking me to present my presentation first, but slowly changed that procedure. I would give them so many different numbers that I knew others wouldn't have to explain my operations. I had gotten so good at my operations, I could tell them how many customers entered each store and on whichever shift they wanted to know about. This was unheard of in that company. By doing this, I gained respect from all of my peers and the management staff. After the respect, they would ask me to have drinks with them, always around me during breaks, calling me just to see how I was doing, etc., totally opposite from the way they treated me at the beginning.

Many times we allow Satan to use our weaknesses because of our unbelief. We cause most of our miseries because we don't trust God enough to believe that He'll do what He'd said He'd do. If we really and honestly believed, we would go on about our business, not worry, and tell Satan to get thee behind us as Jesus did. If we truly have Jesus living in us as we claim, then we have that power. We need to ask God to fix it, believe that He is able, and forget about it. When we stress, worry, etc., we are really telling God we don't believe or trust Him. We tend to lean on our own fleshly understanding and not His true understanding. Faith is the proof you can't see, yet you believe it is already there. Remember, if what you ask for is in God's plan, it's already done. You just have to be patient. I learned that I don't have to be like a crowd to achieve my goals because it's God's will and not the crowd's will that holds my future. Others can't keep us down if God is holding us up. God will take the most unwise and make him/her wise; listen to the stories of our write-offs.

D: SERVING SATAN IN THE MIDST OF GOD'S MERCY

There were many incidents that were showing me that things were getting better in my professional life. It looked like I could begin to breathe easier; I was having a little more happiness doing my job. Even with things going better, there were many times I found my back against the wall and didn't know how I was going to get out. Below are some of those times.

One time we went to New Orleans for a meeting and were checking into this luxury hotel. I kept seeing the people in front of me giving the desk clerk their credit cards, signing for their rooms, then leaving the desk. As the line got shorter coming up to my turn, I started wondering and finally realized that we had to pay for our own rooms. The company would always reimburse us when we had to pay for expenses up front. My problem was I only had about fifty dollars to my name and the rooms for three nights were about four hundred dollars for the total stay. Immediately, I prayed to the Lord that I didn't have the money and I guess I had to be embarrassed in front of all of my peers. I couldn't leave because I didn't have a way back to the airport and probably would lose my job if I didn't show up for the meeting. Every idea I came up with made no sense, nor was there an out in my desperate situation. I was the next one up and prayed hard to the Lord to help me and if it had to be, not to let me be too embarrassed. It was like being placed in a corner with no way out except for what you're looking at and the view I was facing was horrible. When I approached the counter, the clerk asked me my name and started running the total due on her computer. When she told me the total and just as I was about to explain my circumstance, the guy I was rooming with reached his AMEX credit card to her. He told her to put my and his room on his card because there was no reason both of us had to be reimbursed. I was shocked and relieved at the same time, yet silently screaming thanks to God for bailing me out. So we both got our keys and went to our room to unpack.

Later that night we went down on Bourbon Street and partied until the early morning hours. All of the days I was there, my roommate paid for everything for both of us. When I left, I had all of the money I had when I arrived except the amount I spent partying.

Even when we've forgotten about God, He's still watching over us. He could've allowed me to get extremely embarrassed, yet He bailed me out just in the nick of time. He was waiting there to see if I would call upon Him even with Him already having it covered. He knew my roommate was just behind me just as the angel was there when Abraham was about to stab Isaac. Although I thanked God for that blessing, Satan knew I was weak in getting drunk and running after women. Satan showed me that Bourbon Street had both. Even after God had saved me from a terrible embarrassment, I had the nerve to go down to Bourbon Street and party with some of the money God had just saved me. I partied the whole weekend, didn't get into trouble, found my way back to a hotel, and He still protected and had mercy on me. I even had some of my money when I returned home. Immediately after God sent grace and mercy to my rescue, I allowed Satan to take over. I am so glad that God is a forgiving God because if that were man, he would've gotten mad for leaving him, and, for sure, not continue to protect me. It's totally amazing how much God loves us, even when we turn our backs on Him so many times for Satan. Man couldn't have timed my roommate to be in position so perfectly, especially at that second.

One night after a meeting with upper management, all of us went to eat and drink at a bar in the hotel where we were staying. Management was picking up the tab for everything so we drank until all of us got drunk. I was sitting at the table with our female company president and our chairs were turned facing each other. We were drunk and laughing when all of a sudden, the glass I was holding dropped, falling into her lap. I immediately got a napkin and just as I attempted to dry her off, I pulled back after realizing I was about to touch her body. She laughed, wiped herself off, then reached over and kissed me. I didn't know what to do because she was the president and her husband wasn't far away playing pool with another girl. Satan had all of us wrapped up that night. We all got so drunk hardly anyone could function the next day at our meeting.

This could've been a disaster for my career and me personally. I could've gotten fired and sexual harassment could've been filed against me. I could've been trying to find myself a way back home or her husband could've seen the kiss, and there would've been lots of confusion everywhere. Here again, God was watching over me and protected me even in the midst of my mess. Satan puts us in situations that without God being there, could mess up our whole lives.

I also had non-sexual relationships with several of my store managers, which was totally against company policy. I would visit those stores and spend more time with them than the others, which my uninvolved employees would notice. That didn't stop me nor did it slow me down because I was the boss and I felt that I could out-slick the system. Although we never had sex in the stores, it came very close many times. Just at the nick of time, we had just stopped with our acts when someone would walk in on us finding nothing. Each relationship began with an attraction which all of us should've been strong enough but we allowed our lusts to take center stage. I had gotten very comfortable with my actions because I had gotten away with it for so long.

Satan knows what attracts us and will put them right in front of us keeping us confused in our sin. We don't think rationally because it feels better if we are slipping around and believing we're getting away with it. The longer we're allowed to get away with our sin, the bolder we get with our acts. Satan will let us go on and on because he knows the last thing on our minds is to ask God to help us with our lustful feelings.

The females didn't care because they thought they had some type of protection since I was their boss. It had to be God even in this mess because I should've been caught by others walking in on us, answering for sexual harassment charges, threatened by the men in each of their lives, and in an immediate situation of losing my job. All of this would've ruined my life publicly and privately, but God protected me again.

I had a long-term affair with one of the female supervisors who worked under me. She was married, white, smart, and had strong ambitions. Not only initially was I interested in teaching her to be one of the best, but I persuaded her to be my lady. I could tell in my first interview with her that she was attracted to me and that gave me the green light to expose her weakness because I was certainly attracted to her. She was also having some problems in her marriage, which was the excuse for both of our desires. She would always remain with me late at my office.

It began with a kiss but later developed into a romantic and sexual relationship. I was harder on her than any of my other supervisors because I wanted her to stand out so none would suspect our relationship. On out-of-town meetings when our company invited my supervisory staff to attend with me, I would slip into her hotel room when we felt everybody had gone to bed. Those meetings would give her the best excuses to get away from her husband. He had no idea of our relationship, nor did he suspect me being involved with his wife. In fact, when I would be in his presence, we'd act very friendly toward each other (laughing and joking around). It would certainly be hard to portray the boss and supervisor image instead of the lovers when we would be among others at a business function, yet we would always manage to pull it off. Even though we had a relationship, she developed into being the best supervisor I had ever trained. I think others suspected after a while, but didn't have any proof because we were very careful. She was and still is someone very special in my life. I think her kids suspected but didn't say anything because they weren't sure.

Satan had us so bound that we didn't consider anyone else's feelings, just our own. Satan doesn't care and as long as we're serving him, he's satisfied. Never did we even think of God, let alone that we were sinning. I wasn't divorced and neither was she, but that didn't matter to us. Satan will deceive you into thinking your fun will last forever, but it always will come to an end someday. Neither Satan nor us know our future. Many homes and families are broken up because of our actions favoring Satan because we only care about our own lustful actions. Satan set up the attraction knowing that neither of us would resist temptation. He knew both of our marriages were having troubles, so he used that to go against God's law.

Each time we got together and got away with it, there was a certain excitement generated giving us a stronger desire to soon get together again. It would've only taken one time getting caught and both of us would've been terminated.

E: PAYMENT FOR MY SINS

A short time later when things were beginning to look very good for me both personally and professionally, the rug came from under me. I had just ended paying for my bankruptcy and child support, which increased my paycheck tremendously. I thought finally things were beginning to go my way until my supervisor flew down to tell me they were demoting me to a district supervisor. He told me the reasons were because of downsizing and closing slow stores throughout the company. They also included my zone into another zone and selected one of their "good ol' boys" to head the combined zone. He lived closest to the main office and liked the arrangement very much because he thought I would still operate all of my previous stores as before since he was so far away. He told me I was his main man in our territory, but that was because he wanted someone to handle problems. He was my boss yet when we needed him, he would always call back drunk. He was definitely not as knowledgeable of the business, having a title and that was all. He would always try to slip into town without anyone knowing he was coming and would stay in his hotel room most of the time during his stay. I would even get calls from our corporate boss when he wasn't in town to take care of problems my elected boss should've done. It wasn't my fault he lived far from our stores.

The company started to get very bad in their decisions, forgetting the personal touch they originally had with the people. Employees began to become only numbers to them, causing an extreme loss of good people finding jobs elsewhere. I knew I had to save money personally because there was no future for advancement in the company. I prayed to God after having to take my small son with me on robberies and break-ins to give me the time needed to stay home and have enough money to take care of him. There also were visits from the corporate office's "good ol' boy clique" that had no regard for employee feelings.

One evening sitting in my office, I asked God to send me a sign, and if He did, I would pack my things and walk out. A few minutes after asking, my boss's boss called and was very rude in a demanding conversation with me. That was the first time that had ever happened with him, even though many times he wouldn't fight corporate for what was right. We'd find mistakes or problems in print-outs sent by corporate and he would tell us he'd get them corrected, yet would not. I knew then that was the sign I was waiting for, packed up my office, put my things into my car, and drove home. I also deleted all of the forms I created on the company's laptop before leaving.

The next week they called me consistently but I would

never return their calls. They were extremely upset they weren't able to use any of my forms. They were upset that I had deleted all of my numbers off of my laptop. I knew then that my boss and his boss were not going to be able to operate that zone of stores because of the time and efforts the operations required. A few months later, corporate fired my boss, then demoted his boss.

Just when we think we have it all together, but are still serving Satan, our whole world comes tumbling down. It seems when we get to our highest points, we forget who put us there and think we did it on our own. We give God no credit. Many times God has to bring us down from our high just to remind us that He is still in control. It seems like we really don't call on Him until we are down and out. Otherwise, we put Him aside. He will also snatch us down and put us back in the same place to remind us where we came from. We tend to forget the old when He blesses us with the new. Even with Him pulling us down, He still won't allow others to mistreat us and get away with it, especially thinking they're better than us. God also hears us and answers our prayers even during our downfalls that He allows. Our downfalls are determined by how close God wants us to get to Him and dependent upon our obedience to Him. What we must remember during our downfalls is that God is taking us through this for His purpose and not leaving it up to us. He knows we wouldn't follow through, especially if we're comfortable and have knowledge we might lose everything. It's not what my ex-bosses did to me, it's how they did it to me, compounded with the deception used in the process.

We need to treat everyone like we want to be treated and not just during the time when we really need help. Trust me, that same treatment will come back around to us and most times, it'll happen when we least expect it by someone close to us. We will never succeed with the use of mistreatment on others.

I didn't know what I was going to do after walking off of my job, but I knew that if God sent the sign, then I'd be fine. God already knew because there were some other things He wanted me to go through in His plan. I knew that my ex-bosses would fail, be demoted and/or fired because they hid things and had placed themselves far above everyone else. They wanted to be respected because of their titles alone instead of giving out respect before getting it back. Satan had them ignorant of the fact that God was watching every wrong thing they did to His people.

CHAPTER SIX

STILL DROPPING

A: FIRST YEARS OF GOODNESS

My first year and a half of not working was good. I had saved enough money to pay all of my bills each month. I was able to buy Christmas gifts for all of my relatives, and had extra money to blow on my son. I had been blessed with one credit card that had a sufficient credit limit. Life was good, I thought. I felt like just before my savings would run out, I would find a job, continue paying my bills, and build my savings back up. During that time, I had also been blessed with an income tax return and a small profit sharing check. I wasn't serving Satan as much except on special occasions, which definitely included getting drunk. I had lots of time on my hands which helped lift my son's school grades to an "A" average. Before I stopped working, his grades were slipping. This did give me the time I had asked God for. By having so much time during the days when my kid was in school, I began writing the Bible in a poetic form, transcripts of three other books, and a host of poems. As of this writing, I haven't completed the Bible yet but I have completed all of the rest of my writings. It was so amazing because I never had training in writing, yet I finished them in record time with each of them being consistent throughout. Their endings matched their beginnings and their middles without even outlining them before I started.

I submitted all of the books and poems except the Bible writing to publishers and others, but received no real interest in them. I asked God to send me the publishers because He knew I didn't know any or anything about the publishing business. I did receive letters from the offices of Bill Clinton, Coretta King, Convenience Store News, and a few others. I was flattered, but disappointed at the same time. There was even someone in the UK who wrote me for my approval to publish one of my poems in their book and I agreed for the exposure. I sent copies over the internet, yet only got one positive response that wanted me to match their $14K cost to publish one of my books, but I didn't have the money. I began to get very discouraged because there was no interest coming in and I began to question if this was really what God wanted me to do or whether I was really good enough. I even printed everything out, mailed the package out to a company in New York, but got no response.

When I was writing, it looked like there was someone giving me the words that consistently flowed from page to page and chapter to chapter. I didn't want to stop because the words were just pouring out. I was truly enjoying my life and had always promised myself to go to church, yet never did because of one excuse after another. I stayed home most of the time other than going out of town about once a month spending the weekend with my white girlfriend.

My financial situation looked good and my future plans, I thought, would work. I thought I had the best of both worlds, getting closer to God and barely serving Satan. Serving Satan any will take away the special time needed to get closer with God. Even a little time with Satan is going against God's will and commandments. It's like people not thinking it's bad telling a little white lie, yet a lie is a lie no matter what color or how big it is. No matter what, we cannot serve two masters. God answered my prayer giving me the time to spend with my son and He allowed my son's grades to get better. It's always "I" or "we" did this or that and never give credit where it's due. If we could've made things work or happen, we would've already done so without God having to intervene.

The reasons that the books and poems went so well was because it wasn't me, it was God. I didn't have the knowledge or intellect to do such things myself. If God was there when I wrote them, why wouldn't I believe He wouldn't have the publishers also waiting for me? We forget that God doesn't do anything halfway and He gives us "all" of our needs not just part of them. He allowed the letters and poems to reach the high profile desks when normally they wouldn't have because He wanted to show me there was none He couldn't get in touch with. It wasn't the time God had scheduled for the publishing, even though I thought it was and wanted it to be.

Satan knew it was something big brewing, so he had to begin to make me disbelieve and question myself because of my lack of training. He didn't understand that I had the ultimate trainer in God and this was God's plan. Satan wanted me to stop and give up, then I wouldn't need to write of how good God has been.

We can always tell when God is about to do something very big for us because Satan begins to tremble, sending all of his negative powers to stop or discourage us. We most times want to rush God, not realizing that it's His time and not ours. We always ask God to handle things, yet before He does, we tend to stick our hands in there and mess everything up. How can we know what's best for our future when we don't even know our future? There is only One who knows the beginning, ending, and the in-between.

I was still getting drunk and having an affair with a married woman thinking it wasn't that serious. We always think it's just a little this and a little that, yet it is still sin. Sin is like the "white lie" definition, it's still sin no matter how we structure it. God was telling me that this is what He was going to have me do at my later age after going through many good/bad experiences. We have to personally experience things before we can write about them because then it's actual and not second-hand. We write our stories to help others who are going through the same.

B: FINANCES CRUMBLE

After the year and a half ended, I had almost spent all of the money I had saved. When all of it was going out and nothing coming in to replace it, it vanished quickly. Not too long after, I was down to nothing and wondering how I was going to pay my required bills, especially my rent. I first used up all of the credit on my credit card which I couldn't pay back. I didn't want to try to borrow from my relatives because I was too proud and didn't want them to talk about me negatively. My landlord, since I had been there so long and paying on time, worked with me, but it got to a point she was falling behind in her own bills. When I didn't pay, she still had to pay with her own money so she wouldn't lose her house. I applied for unemployment and was denied my benefits. I didn't know what I was going to do because I was getting further behind on my rent and the little money I would get, went toward my utilities. I started looking for work putting in lots of applications, but had no return calls. This was the first time I experienced that you could be over-qualified for positions. I appealed my unemployment and was set up with a phone interview. My boss, his boss, the referee, and I went through the appeal with my ex-bosses lying to the referee. I even caught them in lies, but the referee believed them and denied my appeal.

At this time, I had gotten very desperate and didn't know how to dig myself out of my deep hole. I prayed and pleaded to God for help. Just as soon as my landlord said she couldn't hold out any longer, I appealed again for my unemployment and was approved. I set up a payback plan with my landlord until I caught up, but it didn't leave enough money to catch up on my other bills. I got behind on my car payments and was getting repossession letters warning me what would happen if I didn't catch up.

One cold rainy morning I got up to take my son to school and when we went outside to get into the car, it was gone. It had been repossessed. That was devastating. It hurt me so bad because I only had one year left to pay for it, and had no idea where I could get the money to catch up on the payments. I was catching up on my rent because we needed a place to stay. I allowed the car payments to slide because there was not enough money to go around. I tried different relatives, but none had the money to catch my car payments up.

One night I just gave up and cried out to God. Just around midnight my phone rang and it was my step-mom calling to see how we were doing. After we had small talk, I told her of my car being repossessed and having no answers how I was going to save it. She hesitated and told me to call my cousin and tell her she was sending the past due amount, and I would pay her back when I received the money she was mailing. I immediately called my cousin who agreed to take her house tax money and loan it to me until I received my step-mom's money. The next morning, I called the finance company finding out that was the only day I had to retrieve my car because they were going to take it to a car auction that same day. They agreed to call the repossession place to hold the car for one more day. I got the money, wired it to them, got the release, and picked up my car. I couldn't thank God enough when I was driving it back home. Later that week, I received my step-mom's money and took it right over to my cousin. Everything went fine, yet I still didn't have enough money to pay all of my bills with my unemployment, nor could I find a job. It looked like every job door just closed up on me, even the jobs that seemed anyone could get.

We try to plan our lives and put our own guarantee on it as though we are God Himself. We can make all of the plans we want, but if it doesn't fit with God's plan, it won't work. God has a plan for each of us and who are we to make changes? God will expose us to the worst sufferings just to see if we call on Him, just give up, or try to fix it ourselves. When we try to fix it ourselves, we make our problems worse. It wasn't me that won the unemployment appeal, God already had the win set up for me.

Sometimes we think when one thing gets a little better, everything is going to get better and then something else gets worse. We ask ourselves when it will end because we're going one step forward and two steps back. When this happens we tend not to cry out as much for God as we did when we gave up. He wants us to realize that only He can pull us out of those terrible situations. Our praise and cries decrease after He has brought us out of bad situations. He's also testing the strength of our faith with the back-to-back problems. We know He's there because He shows us by bringing us out at the nick of time after we give up. Look how He handled the car situation; just as I gave up, He heard my cry and came through with the phone call from my step-mom. Also, the very next day they were going to take the car to be auctioned off and God stepped in, saving it. We place ourselves on the edge with worry and stress. We always say we believe in God, but that's a lie because giving up on the edge is disbelief. Giving up is also mistrust in God and not believing in God's promises. Many things we want to happen don't because it's not good for us or God has something better for us in the future. Maybe we wouldn't be able to handle such a blessing God wants to give us at our expected time and God knows that. We need to learn to completely turn it over to God, trust Him, and praise Him in our good and the bad circumstances believing it's His will.

God wanted me flat broke with no job so I could go to the next stage of His plan. God knew if I got a job, I would've gotten back to being comfortable, possibly gone back to my old ways with Satan, stopped all of my writings, and wouldn't have experienced the sufferings. He also wanted me to see who would come to my rescue, including my relatives, when I really needed someone, if no more than to just listen. When God orders our footsteps, He does each and everything for a reason.

C: ENTIRE BOTTOM FALLS

Just when I thought things had gone from worse to bad, my life turned worse again with a steady downward turn. I had no money coming in, spent all of the money I had, didn't have food, and the bills including my rent had gotten behind again. The bottom started falling out of my life as the series of things below began to happen.

To relieve some of my pain, I turned to the things that eliminated my bad thoughts. My son and I drove to my aunt's birthday party where I got wastefully drunk. When the party was over, my relatives tried to get me to spend the night at their home, but I decided against it. I felt that I could make it home not realizing how drunk I really was or remembering I wasn't the only one riding home. I put the one that meant the world to me and myself in danger when I made that decision.

About halfway home, I began to see blurs and had to ask my son to help me see how to drive going home. There should've been no way I should've made it home, especially with all of the highway overpasses we had to drive past. When we got home, I stumbled inside of the house and we both went to bed.

The next morning when I got sober, I thought about the

chance of me killing my son and/or myself because of my drunkenness. At that point, the drinking wasn't worth placing anyone else's life in my drunken hands. From that point, I gave up alcoholic beverages and never looked back even up to this writing. Immediately reality set in and after forgetting my problems for a while, my problems were still there. My drunkenness didn't eliminate anything.

Satan knew one of my weaknesses was alcohol and knew that things had gotten so bad I wouldn't refuse his invitation. Satan convinces us to just drink a few to give us enough time to forget about our problems for a while. What he doesn't tell us is with our problems, one drink will lead to many more, resulting in drunkenness. Satan catches us most time when we're on our way to the bottom because he knows that's when we are at our weakest. He also knows we're weak in the mind and strong-willed during drunkenness, causing us to make decisions we shouldn't. We always feel that we're "not that drunk" even with our body actions proving differently. Even though I was in my drunken stage, God still protected my son and me driving home. If not for God's grace, we probably would've driven off of one of the overpasses, killing us both.

What Satan didn't figure into his plans was that I would fix one of my weaknesses the very next day by quitting alcohol. All of our habits we think we need professional help with are only in our minds and can be eliminated by asking God to remove those desires from us. If God removes the desire we'll have no need for a habit, nor will its presence make a difference. Also, God's services don't cost us a dime.

Many times I didn't have money to buy cigarettes, my son's school needs, or just miscellaneous items. Each time this would happen, a first cousin would stop by the house and before leaving, give us a few dollars. It had gotten to the point that I would tell my son I felt that she was coming by, and she would come by that same day. She also started loaning me money to pay my rent, most times the day before my landlord would come to collect.

One day we needed money so bad, we didn't know what we were going to do. My cousin was walking around a track at a park and said she didn't know why, but something told her to come by our house to check on us. She said it was so powerful that she somehow was made the drive by our house on her way home. After she got there we sat there talking about God, her problems, and my problems for a long time. Before she left, she went into her pocket and gave me some money, which was a little more than the amount we needed. This spurred a few more of my cousins to help out as much as they could.

I remember one day I needed some specific cleaning supplies with no money to purchase them and my aunt called telling me to stop by her house. When I got there, she gave me a few food packages, meats, and the exact cleaning supplies that I needed. My cousin helped me more than any other relative and did so until I moved. She was definitely there in my corner when I really needed someone.

Some relatives or friends will only help others in need to make them look big to others. Some help because other close ones take center stage and they want part of that stage even if they are not sincere about helping. Some only help because of guilt they will feel among other friends or relatives. Helping others in need because of personal or boastful motives does not please God. If we can't help because of our hearts, we don't need to help at all. There is no doubt that God was using my cousin as our "ram in the bush." When I needed something, I didn't worry because I just expected it from God because I believed in His promises. He will never leave nor forsake us! My cousin was just His vessel. There was no way my cousin could've known I needed money, nor my relatives could know which supplies I needed, but God knew. I told her, when she was about to settle for a car less than the one she wanted, she needed to pray, be patient, and not settle for second best. I was convinced by her sincere help for us, that God was using her and He would give her that desire of her heart.

After a few disappointments in shopping for the one she wanted and having patience to wait on God, He gave her the exact one she wanted, down to the color. He even gave her the payments she wanted along with extras she didn't even ask for. That's the kind of God we serve. Not only did I need my cousin, she needed me because God had a message for her about her troubles. The strong feelings she had were guidance from God so both of us could get together for each other. God blesses us to bless others, yet most times when we get ours, we don't want to share.

One day my son was hungry and we only had two eggs left in the house to cook. I was also hungry, but I did without so my son could eat even knowing that the two eggs would only help a little. I didn't know what I was going to feed him later, yet I had to think of the present. After I fried the eggs and he ate, I began to wash the dishes. I again thought about my child not having anything to eat later and started crying, screaming out to God to help us. Just as I was telling God I was hungry too, something told me to look out of the front room window. When I did, I saw my three stepkids opening up the trunk of an SUV and each one started bringing bags and bags of groceries into our house.

My stepson had come home on military leave and had decided to grocery shop for me. All I could do was jump for joy and thank God for the blessing.

He's an "on-time" God and proves He knows our situation at all times. The time it took my kids to leave their mom's house, drive to the grocery store, shop for the groceries, and drive up to the front of my house would've at least taken two hours. This was two hours prior to my cry out to God for help. This means that God was already supplying my need even before I had asked. That's why Jesus says we don't need to pray a long prayer because the

Father knows our needs even before we ask. He may not come when we want Him, but He's always right on time. The only One who knew we were hungry and had no food was God, so those who are in doubt that He's real have to believe because of this story, especially its timing. Man couldn't have set this thing up to happen just after I prayed. It wasn't mere coincidence that my kids went to the store because they didn't even know our situation.

One weekend I just needed to get away from my problems and my son had already gone for the weekend. The pressure had really gotten to me, so I made a date with the married white girl who lived out of town. She couldn't come to pick me up so I had to drive up there. My only problem was I had no money to buy gas, etc., and I didn't want to look unmanly asking her to pay for my expenses. I had bought a riding lawnmower earlier that year and I decided that I would sell it for the money. This lawnmower was a gift from God by the way I received it and I really didn't want to get rid of it. I had already lost my horseshoe ring, a large television, gold bracelet, two cameras, etc., to the local pawnshop after needing the money for bills and food. The lawnmower was the only thing left that I thought I could get money for quickly.

I put it out on the front lawn with a "for sale" sign on it that morning, but only got a couple of people who showed interest. I also called a friend of mine who showed interest for his daughter's husband but wasn't sure. I had a certain time I had to leave and needed to sell it before that time. As the day was drawing to an end, there was nobody coming by and I started to get depressed even though I had asked God for help. The closer it got to the time, the more frantic I got, deciding that what I was about to do wasn't of God and He wasn't going to help me. About an hour before leaving, I looked outside and it was my friend coming to look at the mower. At first it looked like he wasn't going to buy it because he didn't know how he'd deliver it to his house. As he was thinking about it, I was praying to God for help. Finally, about thirty minutes later, he decided to buy it, go get his truck to transport it, and with my help, take it home. He also paid me less than the amount I was asking for it, but I didn't care because I just needed to get away. As I was helping him, I was thanking God. After we did everything, I was able to drive out on time and instead of paying that money on bills, I allowed my emotions to decide my least priority. I had a good time, yet when I got back home, the same problems were still waiting for me.

Many times when we're so depressed and overwhelmed with our problems, Satan puts our greatest ungodly desires in front of us. He makes us believe those desires are the answer for our immediate emotional need. We are so vulnerable and weak, we most always accept his invitation rather than wait in pain for God. It seems like Satan's way feels better at the time because we don't want to think about the future. We just want what we think is relief from that feeling right away. God prolongs what we want to do so we'll realize it's wrong and decide not to do it.

He also reminds us of our past bad experiences trying to get us to make the correct choices because if it didn't work back then, chances are it won't work this time either. He is so gracious He allows it, even knowing when it's all over we're still in the same old spot. God always gives us a choice before we do or say things and always reminds us if it's wrong or not. Even here, God allowed me to have my desire.

Sometimes God will remove His hands allowing us to have our desire just to show us it wasn't worth it in the end. Even in my mess, God was still there answering my prayers. Satan loves it when we make quick and irrational decisions because he knows we're not thinking things through completely. Satan will have us so confused, it's like a drug addict being on the edge, not interested in tomorrow.

There have been so many times that I promised my landlord her rent money even before I knew where I was going to get it. One time I was $300 short and she needed the money the following day because she was behind on her own bills. I knew I had to get it from somewhere and I walked in the backyard praying to God, yet everyone I would call wasn't able to help me. I even called some so-called friends who lived out of town, but to no avail. I tried to call my landlord several times leaving messages for her to call me back, but she never would. I knew at that point that I was in serious trouble of getting kicked out of the house. So I prayed and prayed until finally I just gave up to let the chips fall where they may. Later that afternoon, I received a visit from my ex-wife who had walked into the house with a white envelope. She opened it and pulled out a check that was sent from my stepson sending both of us $250. I told her my problem and she left later bringing me my share back in cash. I was still short and I went to the grocery store, cashed a $60 personal check for cash, then returned home. I didn't have the money in the bank, but that just bought me some time before I could try and borrow the money to put it back in to catch the check. My landlord came the next day and I paid my rent. Of course, I could never get the money to catch the personal check and it bounced costing me an additional $60.

Again, I didn't completely trust God. He had the money on the way from the time I was calling others who didn't have it or just didn't want to loan me any money. I was sitting there worried, praying, depressed, etc., when God already had it done. God was telling me that day to tell my landlord I'd have the money because He knew that my stepson had already sent it and how long it would take to get to me. God even knew which day to make my ex-wife come by my house with the envelope. If God knows the number of hairs on each of our heads, why wouldn't we believe He knows every detail of our lives and needs? Allowing Satan to run things only get us in compounded trouble because we're not thinking straight, but confused.

Why didn't I trust God to send me the other $50 I needed for my total rent? He'd already sent me the largest amount unexpectedly, so why wouldn't He send the balance? I strongly believe that before that night was over, God would've sent me the other money because He promised to supply "all" of my needs and not just some. I thanked Him for the $250, but then I didn't trust Him any more and leaned to my own understanding when I went and cashed the personal check that bounced. It bounced costing me double because I gave up my trust in God and He was showing me the results. If I would have continued trusting Him, it wouldn't have cost me a dime. Trust God to do the whole job!

D: EVICTION TO NOWHERE

Well, finally, the entire bottom fell out. I found myself crying and speaking to God in a church parking lot on a rainy day. I couldn't understand why God hadn't completely pulled me out of my terrible situation. There was no more robbing Peter to pay Paul, borrowing from friends or relatives, holding off my landlord for her rent money, money to pay my utilities to keep them on, and no more nothing. I was holding onto the edge of the bottom and slipping to fall through. I had gotten behind on my car payments and had to hide the car in the backyard at night so it wouldn't be repossessed. This time, the company would only accept the payoff price and nothing less in order for me to keep the car. One evening my landlord called and told me she had to have all of the back rent money immediately because now the future of her house was threatened. She said if I couldn't come up with the money by the next morning, she had to evict my son and me. She told me she wished she had another choice, but she didn't because she had to get us out so she could rent the house right away so she wouldn't lose her house.

I told her that I understood and that it didn't look good of me coming up with the money. I prayed and prayed that night, but the next morning, there was no money. When she called and I told her I didn't have the money, she told me I had three days by law to get out. There was no way I could get the house packed and us moved within that time. I had no money, boxes, truck, place to store everything and the only thing I could do was to pray. I didn't even know where I was going to go to live. My relatives didn't offer and when they did, I could tell they really didn't want us to interrupt their lives. My friends were scarce or they didn't answer my calls. I didn't have money to get my son and me a room to stay in. I didn't know what to do but pray. I refused to cry because it wouldn't have changed anything anyway.

That afternoon, which was July 13, I was sitting on a bench outside wondering what I was going to do and playing with a stick. I looked at the stick and had configured "MC" out of it. I asked God what it meant. Immediately, the phone rang and it was my ex-wife just calling to check on us. I went back outside and instantly it came to me that the initials of the stick were my ex-wife's initials and she was born on the thirteenth. I still didn't know what it meant or why that happened.

That night after I explained the situation to my son and he went to sleep, I sit in the kitchen looking at all of the stuff I had to pack. I was talking to God and hoping there was another answer other than having to move, but something told me this was the way it would be. It also told me to get trash cans or whatever I could find and start packing immediately because I was going to leave that house. I got up and started doing just that and realized there was no way I could do it all within three days. I told God that I needed at least until that following Saturday. I packed until I got so tired that I had to go to bed.

The next morning I got up, sent my son to school, started packing, and put stuff in bags or anything I could find. I packed all day, fed my son dinner, then sat down to rest before getting started again because I only had two days left. While sitting there, I heard something at the front door. I went to the door to see what it was, and found a piece of paper stuck in the door's handle. When I opened it, it was my written eviction paper letting me know when I had to be out of the house. I was elated thanking God because the day on the paper was the Saturday that I prayed for. I set a plan of placing things I didn't need in the front yard to sell, packing/cleaning one room at a time within the days left, and positioning everything for an easy move out of the house. But I had no money to pay for a truck, a storage unit, gas for the vehicles. I had no money to keep them from turning off the phone or lights, no money to get my driver's license renewed, etc. I was in bad shape even with the extra time God had given me.

The day before my time was up, my first ex-wife wired me money for the storage. I went straight down and leased the last unit that would hold all of my stuff. In fact, another man changed his mind for that unit while I was standing there and that was the only one left big enough to hold all of my stuff.

The very last day I sold all of my excess stuff, got two free trucks for transport. I had gotten everything out of the house cleaning each room, and had an extra $200 in my pocket when I left on time that Saturday. Even when nothing was selling at my yard sale, the last morning, God had told me to stop at this corner flea market lot to ask them to come and buy what they wanted. At first, the guy said he didn't want anything and went to his truck to leave, but turned around and bought two truckloads of my excess. Then all of a sudden, all of my neighbors started coming over and bought most of the rest of my excess. All of the stuff I had left just fit perfectly into the storage unit. My ex-wife had invited us to stay with her until I got up on my feet.

A bandage on an open wound will only last so long and after it continues to peel off with the wound not getting any better, sooner or later we have to go to a doctor. They need to close (stitch) that wound completely so we don't have to worry about that one any more and start fresh, giving it time to heal. God knew it was within His plan for us to get out of that house and nothing I said or prayed would change that. God had already given me until that Saturday when my landlord told me we were being evicted because the papers had already been typed up that day.

The very next day the paper was delivered and I didn't ask God for the additional time until the evening after talking to the landlord. When I received the paper with the additional time, I knew then God had His hands on my move.

Even when all odds are against us, God comes through and He won't put more on us than we can bear. Every prayer I prayed, He answered it including no utility was turned off until two days after I left the house. I had called all the companies and asked for them to cut each off that Monday after the Saturday, and all agreed to give me the time. That was nobody but God because I was really behind on each one of the companies and under normal circumstances, they would've cut them off the day I called, especially when I told them I was moving.

I never would've gotten rid of all of my excess if I wasn't obedient to God, yet would've had to leave a lot of good stuff in the house. Not only did God give me one truck to move, He gave me two and it didn't cost me a single penny. Also, God made that guy who wanted to rent that last storage unit change his mind at the last minute allowing me to walk up right after him and rent it. God knew what I needed and held it for me. I was also going to wait until the next day to rent it after I got the money, but God told me to go down that night and now I can see why. God had also already set up that flea market man and my neighbors to buy all of my excess because He wanted me to trust Him taking care of everything. I told Him after the first few days nothing sold that He would have to do this not knowing He had it already scheduled.

We tend to rush God when things don't happen the time we want them to and we don't trust that He knows exactly what He's doing. We are quick to allow Satan to tell us that things are not going to work out because of our grave position and we forget that there's nothing too hard for God. I had to allow God to guide me the entire way because I had no other choice. God already knew how it would turn out, even down to staying with my ex-wife (stick sign). I alone packed a three-bedroom house in five days having nothing, I thought, to pack it in, but God even had that figured out. We count God out too many times. I had nothing but a prayer to start, but finished with much more.

CHAPTER SEVEN

FROM SKILLET TO FRYING PAN

A: STRICT LIVING CONDITIONS

My son and I moved in with my ex-wife and my stepdaughter not knowing what our living conditions were going to be. Early on I found out they were not going to be as I had expected. All of our belongings (clothes, shoes, supplies, etc.) had to fit into one small closet. We had to move around things just to get the things we needed. I tried to organize it for what we needed from first to last, but the closet was too small. The hanging clothes were so tight, it was extremely hard to get out or to keep our clothes unwrinkled. We had to leave a lot of our small useable items in our suitcases because of lack of space, bringing the whole thing out when we needed something. It was horrible to live like this. We slept on a mattress we placed on the living room floor each night and had to pick it up and store it behind the front door each morning. We were chastised if we left it down on the floor too long, or didn't reposition the furniture back as we found it, or didn't clean the floor after picking it up. We were limited to short showers because of reminders that we weren't paying the water bill. I limited my showers to about three times a week to conserve on water. I had to slip and wash our clothes because of the water bill and being unable to buy detergents or Clorox. I would mostly wait until she was gone to wash all of our clothes and would wonder why, especially when I was the one who gave her the washer and dryer free. This procedure was also done with the ironing of our clothes. My son had to put up his game machine just right or else he'd get yelled at. I would wash all of the towels daily keep the house clean, cook, wash dishes, and mow the yard trying to work for my stay, but that still wasn't good enough.

Relatives and friends will welcome you into their home and make you think you're really welcomed. It doesn't show how sincere they are until you accept their invitation and move in on their previous arrangements. That's when their true colors appear with quietness, frowns, making known their financial problems in loud voices, whisperings, spacing themselves, etc. The demands were high, but we had to accept them because we had nowhere else to go. There were more closets in the two-bedroom house, but we weren't offered additional space. My ex-wife and stepdaughter could've bedded together and given the other bed to my son and me, but that didn't happen either. If we weren't there, the bills would've been the same anyway and needed to be paid. Most of the washing and ironing were her own son's clothes anyway. You would've thought she would've been glad because this would've been one way she could've made up for some of the years she wasn't there for him.

People soon forget when someone has helped them in the past. I gave them a life that most people would dream about (two-story home, personal car, all utilities they wanted. I sold vacations each year for requested Christmas gifts, helped raise three babies not my own blood, paid credit cards, etc., totally opposite from the life they were living). If nobody else saw the way we were being treated, God did and I know He wasn't happy. Relatives on my side would drop off, only when they felt guilty, cigarettes or cigarette money, then talk about me later. We must forgive them because God has a way of putting them in your same position. It was really hard when my son would cry out he wanted to leave, but we had nowhere to go. It was bad enough treating me this way, but to treat your own blood youngest son this way is unheard of. Satan had her so far gone and confused, she couldn't think straight.

B: SOCIAL STRUCTURES

My ex-wife had male friends who most likely had a problem with her ex-husband living in her house. They probably were making decisions for her concerning my son and me, especially when she was depending on them to pay her bills. She bragged about this "hustle" many times and seemed to be very proud of it. Many times she would leave out of town with one for three to four days at a time, which would give us some peace for those few days. She'd only call when she was out of town just to see if my stepdaughter was being taken care of and eating. Most times my son and I would have to wait until they weren't around to get something to eat. She would get onto my son if sometimes he would eat too much or just go into the refrigerator too often or eat the cereal that belonged to someone else. It had gotten so bad that I would hesitate and limit my son's eating habits because I didn't want anything said. I felt like I had to cook more than I should just to pay for my kid having to eat. I hardly ate anything because I wasn't putting any food into the house, yet my son's name gave them more food stamps. Sometimes I would be so hungry I would wait until they were asleep, then slip into the refrigerator and pinch off some food.

On my ex-wife's good days, she would invite me to eat, but most times I would say I wasn't hungry because I didn't want to be talked about eating the food her men friends had purchased. Many times my son would be asleep, but I would be awakened with them thinking I was asleep and her men friends would bring them food they had bought from a restaurant. All of them including my stepkids would go into my ex-wife's bedroom, close the door, and eat without at least waking my son up to join them. I would be so hungry and knew that my son was, but at least he was asleep. The smell from the food would circulate all around the room where we were sleeping making my hunger much more intense. She would call her men friends to bring hamburgers, etc., only for her and the kids, none for me.

One day I was sitting at the kitchen table after one of these practices and the food bag was on the table in front of me. Her friend that bought the food came through and looked into the bag making sure all of the food had been distributed so none would come to me. Although I was hungry, I didn't say a word. She had one friend named John who was more sympathetic and kind to me. He was a good guy who worked hard, loved my stepkids, was timid with her, and was used by my ex-wife just to get what she wanted. He would leave his job just to satisfy her material needs and he was cursed out if he refused. Many times when I needed cigarettes, John would just show up with a pack or offer me some out of his pack. Her other friends spoke to me, but the tension told me they weren't happy with my son and me being there. All she and her girlfriends wanted to do was party—when they wanted to get away from their men friends. This was almost a daily habit with them, especially in the evenings. I remember even walking at least four miles to a grocery store for food if there was none in the house. She would only ask me to go if she or my stepdaughter wanted to eat.

My ex-wife failed to remember all of the times late at night when she and my stepdaughter were hungry, that she would call me and I would take them half of the food I had in my house. Where were those men friends then? She also failed to remember all of the times she brought her dirty clothes over to my house, washing and drying without limits. I had to pay my utilities at that time also and didn't ask her for a dime.

This was certainly Satan's den surrounded with his followers. Not wanting me to eat was one thing, but treating our son that way was horrible. When they asked Jesus who would be the most important in the Kingdom of Heaven, He pulled this little boy and put him in the midst of them. How can you treat someone whom you birthed that way, especially when you hadn't taken care of him for seven years? She didn't understand that mistreating us was really mistreating God. Satan confuses us to forget about our help when we are in need and not allowing anyone to interrupt what we feel will last forever, especially if it seems like happiness.

Satan allows us to have only selective memory. My son and I were thorns in Satan's side because he knew I was seeking God more, bringing Him into all of my situations. No matter how much they threw at us, we were going to make it through, yet sometimes I wondered. So Satan tried to make our living conditions so miserable that we would break and move on. One thing we had going in our favor was that God placed us there for His purpose and not Satan's.

Lot and his family were the only ones in Sodom and

were saved before the destruction. They say "blood is thicker than water," but not when we allow Satan to run our lives. You soon tend to get jealous of her friends and ask why, especially knowing how sinful they are. That's something you try to control because the Bible teaches us not to be envious or jealous, but it's hard because of the bad position you're in. We always must treat others the way we want to be treated, even if the same isn't shown back to us. It probably was hard for my ex-wife's male friends to see me each time they came there, but God placed me there for His reason. Maybe He wanted them to see His face each time they came in sin, possibly making them think about what they were doing. When they would slip food in the house and we were hungry, God sustained our appetite where our stomachs seemed full. God said if there is someone hungry, feed them; if there is someone thirsty, give them a drink. Our daily living conditions were horrible and it was only by the grace of God that we managed, even emotionally.

C: HATEFULNESS

Our lives later got worse when my oldest stepdaughter and her kids moved into the house. She lost her apartment and had problems with her babies' daddy while dating another guy. Now there were more mouths to feed, more washing, etc., which created a nastier attitude from my ex-wife. She didn't want my son, my stepdaughter, her grandkids, or me living there. She had forgotten that she had to live with my stepdaughter without paying anything just before she moved into the house we were living in. She and my younger stepdaughter stayed with my older stepdaughter almost a year. She also forgot about me driving about twenty miles each day taking my younger stepdaughter to school and picking her up with her not buying any gas. The only times she would treat me a little better was when she needed to drive my car to meet with her friends. I wouldn't care so much because it was better for me when it was gone because I knew it was a matter of time before it would get repossessed. Fear would come all over me each time I would see a tow truck riding in the neighborhood. I was scared to park it anywhere thinking it would be gone when I got back to it. When they would shop for groceries, they would only buy what they wanted to eat even though we were authorized a portion because they included my son's name. When there was a birthday party, they would spend about three-fourths of the stamps on the party, then suffer with the other one-fourth toward the end of the month. We could always count on getting cursed out by my ex-wife at least once a day when she was at home.

My older stepdaughter and I would literally have a patio meeting almost every Saturday discussing when we were going to leave and where/how were we going to get bill money. She would give my son and me a time limit to go stay with my relatives even knowing they too didn't want us. One time my older stepdaughter and me got so mad, we reminded my ex-wife about when we were there when she was hungry and needed a place to live. That reminder didn't faze her at all because most times, she would have a hangover from the night before. It was unbearable but reality was we didn't have anywhere else to go. She would always close herself into her bedroom so she wouldn't have to see us. My ex-wife would go out of town for a few days with a man friend and when she would return, she would look for things to pick on us about. She would always say she was leaving because she couldn't stand being in her own house with all of us there. It would really get bad when the bills would become due and she had to ask her men friends for the money. That would be a typical example of "hell on earth."

She would always forget about the times my older stepdaughter would get money from her boyfriend to pay a bill or the times when I would get a little money toward the bills.

One day the water got cut off and I rode a bike about six miles round trip to cash a check I'd received from my stepmother. When I returned, I rode the bike through the neighborhood until I found the waterman, paid him, and got the water turned back on that day. Still none of what we did was ever good enough because we would still get cursed out.

She also forgot about the time I not only got her a home phone in my name, but paid the bills up until not long before I moved in with her. They would also go out to the stores to shop, then restaurants afterwards, but would never take my son, knowing he wanted to go. He would cry and I know he felt the mistreatment because he would always ask me when were we going to leave.

Many Christians forget where we came from and the people along the way who were there for us. When God allows us to do better, we forget who pulled us out of our bad situations. Satan will trick us into thinking we'll never be in our previous bad situations again. He'll make us believe we'll never need the ones we're mistreating again. Never burn the bridge that allowed you to cross after you get over to the other side because you may need to use that same bridge again. The grass many times is not greener on the other side, we just get deceived by Satan.

My ex-wife was so deceived by Satan, she really meant the cursing, threats, and nastiness that came out of her mouth frequently. The Bible teaches us it's not what goes in that defiles a man, but what comes out. Satan doesn't care who you hurt as long as he's using your weakness to serve him. It's a terrible feeling knowing you are living in a place where no one wants you and there's nowhere else you can go. Also, having to live that life day in and day out seemed like forever and seeing no hope in sight was horrible. I really wasn't as concerned for myself as I was for my son because he didn't deserve his treatment. Greater is He that's in you than he that's in the world.

I also had to remember they spit on and talked about

Jesus. The Bible says we must die daily and this is a typical example. Being nasty to others only escalates in the non-positive environments, especially when tensions are already high. Do unto others as you would have them do unto you. Satan only gives us a "one-track" mind and all of our thoughts are pointed toward him. Women who put their men friends before their own flesh and blood children have seriously void and confused minds. Nobody but God should be the only One above our children. How can a woman carry a child for nine months inside of her, then turn her back because of someone she only knows second-best? My ex-wife didn't even consider that I accepted three of her children and gave them everything I was able to give, neither of them had my blood. *Touch not my anointed or do my prophet no harm!*

D: DAILY ENVIRONMENT

To get away from all of the hatred, I would walk my son to school and my stepdaughter to the bus stop each morning. When I got back, I would get my Bible, poems, and other writings from inside of the house and set all of it in a chair on the carport. Then I would walk this certain route from the alley in back of the house to the corner store and back to the house the same way. I would talk to God during the entire route, crying out to Him with my situations. When I would get back, I would stay under that carport from morning until late evening even after it had gotten dark. That place was where I found peace, and the only times I went into the house during the day was when I needed to use the restroom. I sat out there when it was cold, rainy, or hot because I felt very safe there. Many times she would scream from the backdoor cursing me or yelling out whatever she had a problem with. Every time I would get so stressed that I couldn't bear it, I would walk my same route just to ease my pain.

Just at the time when I thought I was losing my mind and was ready to go anywhere other than there, a wrecker came and repossessed my car. It was strange because I really didn't get upset, even seeing it pull away and knowing I'd never see it again. All I felt was that I was really stuck at a place I hated and the worst part, I didn't know how long I'd be there.

All day I would read the Bible and write poetry describing all of my pains. I had to express my feelings somehow and writing was what I enjoyed doing. I met and ministered to a lot of people who were hurting and one became a close friend. His name was Joe and we met when he was walking his dog. He saw me writing poetry about the Bible, questioned me on how was I doing it, and wanted to know more about Jesus. He started stopping by every day telling me of his experiences and wondering whether they were of God. When I would walk and didn't have any cigarettes, I would pick up old ones someone had dropped or just thrown away. The coins that I would find along the way, after a while, would add up enough so I could buy a pastry at the corner store. That eased my hunger for a little while. I would eat it behind the dumpster while I was at the store and thank God.

As time went by, I had lost so much weight that you could hold my drooping skin on my arms, legs, face, and stomach in your hands. Every time I would get so frustrated, I would want to give up and God would tell me to just trust Him. All of the people around the alley knew me as the walking man with the stick, but they knew there was something different about me. Seven days a week and several times a day, I would walk, crying out to God. The only one I truly trusted was God. When I would finally go into the house and there would be trouble or negative words said, I would take my writings and sit on the front porch or go back to the carport.

Sometimes my relatives would pass over me without saying a word. Sometimes it would be so cold I had to walk just to keep warm but I would not go into the house. Sometimes it would be so hot, the sun would continue baking my skin to a dark tan and I would compare the brightness behind my clothes with my exposed darker skin. When it would rain, I would move my chairs around to dry places. My ex-wife's men friends and girlfriends would drive into the carport, get out, saying some degrading statements, and walk into the house. Sometimes they would just walk around me without saying a word, most times including my ex-wife. There was a lot of crying and praying under that carport. Many times when I couldn't sleep because I would look at my son suffering through this, I would get up and go outside under the carport to pray.

Everyone needs his/her own closet for an intimate one-on-one with God. The carport and walks were my closets because those are the places I felt closest to God. Those places were where I knew He heard my cries. When I was in either of my closets, Satan had no authority or say. I could certainly say, "Satan, get thee behind me," as Jesus did when Satan tried to tempt Him one of those three times.

It seemed like I was always on another planet when I walked my routes because there was nobody but God and me. Satan tried to get to me when my ex-wife screamed from the door cursing but it didn't bother me. When Joe and the others came down the alley wanting answers, I knew God had sent them. If I am lifted up, I'll draw all men unto me and He was lifted up every day all day under that carport and during the alley walks. When the people would stop, they were stopping for the peace that was there. When they would look at me sitting under the carport not knowing why they stopped, they were looking for God because almost all of them had some serious problems. God was still on the throne when my car got repossessed and probably the reason I didn't get upset was because I was convinced that it was God's will. God knew that I was at the point of my frustration wherein a few more days of that frustration, and I would've loaded up my son, whatever could fit, and left. Even if I had to stay with different people each day, it would've been better than where I was.

My friend out of town wanted me to come there and start over which is probably the place I would've ended up. God knew I had to go through this terrible suffering to be able to help someone down the line and to make me get closer to Him. I wasn't able to put it off any longer because where I was, it was just Him and me. All of the previous times, I would always put someone else or something else before God and He wasn't having it this time. He said that He's a jealous God and to put nothing before Him. God has a way to bring us down so far that we have no choice but to call on Him. He knew if He took my transportation, I had to stay there to fulfill His purpose.

Daily stress is an illness and will destroy your physical and mental body to the extent you will look and sound like someone you're not. Look what they did to Jesus' beaten body and Job's body with boils, yet both encountered those long-sufferings and survived. Are we any better than those two? God let me know when I was getting evicted with the stick initials of my ex-wife. Looking back, He fixed everything I needed to clear the path to get to the suffering at her house.

How are we going to truly help the lost if we have never been lost ourselves? There's a difference in being told how to fix something and actually knowing how to fix it because you've fixed it before. I really didn't worry about my ex-wife's friends' attitudes toward me because I knew they weren't taunting me, they were taunting God. My ex-wife's men friends weren't rejecting me from eating, they were rejecting God. My ex-wife didn't curse me out, she was cursing out God. I could've gotten nasty or into an argument with them, but that's what Satan wanted me to do. Love thy neighbor as thyself. Once you understand that people love to kick you when you're down, it won't bother you to still be nice to them. At that point, they'll think you're crazy and sooner or later leave you alone. It's one thing when you hope, wish, believe, or think God is with you, but altogether different when you know He's there. *Yea do I walk through the valley of the shadows of death, I shall fear no evil, for Thou art with me!*

E: GOD'S PRESENCE

When God is present, He'll show Himself through speaking to you, signs, unexpected gifts, and any other way where there is no other explanation for what just happened. Below are some of the things that happened to me proving God's presence is real and He was definitely there with me. There were many more than described below, but this is enough to show there was no other explanation but God.

A few days after I began to walk the alley and talk to God, I would notice these pennies in front of me. At first, I didn't think anything of them because I was so intent in my fellowship with God. Then each day there would be more and more pennies, which told me I needed to pay attention. One day when I walked up to one, I thought about what I was just talking to God about and it was in a question form. Instantly I snapped, realizing that God was answering me back with the coins. Since then and up to this present writing, He confirms my thoughts and questions with coins. These coins have been in places that no other person would've normally seen, but He showed them to me. It's like He told me when there was one in the grass, behind a bus stop bench, on the pay phone ledges, etc.

God shows us signs which most times we think are coincidence or luck. When you ask God to order your steps and truly believe He's doing so, there are no such things as coincidence and luck. These are signs God is trying to get your attention or tell you something. God will actually speak to you, but you have to know His voice even if you don't want to hear what He has to say. Sometimes we hear Him and ignore His message because that's not what we want to hear. We then say that wasn't God talking to us because it didn't fit our fleshly desires. Along with speaking to me, our other communication was the coins.

Many times we are so distressed when talking to Him, we can't hear because we're praying so hard. These are the times He shows me a coin to let me know that He hears my cry and that He's with me. During my walks with God, He knows what I'm going to say and exactly where I'm going to say it, so He leaves me a coin at each of those spots. He also knows what is ailing our hearts and He will give us signs or messages through whatever means necessary and we know it when it happens. He'll also answer our pressing questions through revelations. We may not want to see the answer. He will also give us signs through our dreams, but we need a godly person like Joseph to interpret the message. When something is very heavy on my heart, God will wake me up between 2 to 3 a.m. just so we can spend a little time together. We know it's Him because He's the only One who has the power to wake us up each morning.

I've proved many times to people who weren't walking in the spirit and thought I was crazy when I told them about the coins. I proved it to a pastor, my son and his friend, and various others including my friend Joe from the alley. When I told Joe, he challenged me to walk a route that he picked, and if God put two pennies in front of him, he would believe. I accepted his challenge and as soon as we got started, I told him God would put five pennies in front of his feet. When we got to the very first corner, there was a penny at his foot. I asked him if he was going to pick up the penny God left him and he was amazed. A few steps more, there was another one by his foot and this time he was so amazed, he said we didn't have to find any more because he believed.

We finished his route and when we got back, we had found five pennies in front of Joe. He knew that there was no way that could've happened unless it was God.

Another incident was when I told my son and his friend that God would leave a penny in back of a bus stop bench after finding two representing the Father and Son. The other one would be for the Holy Ghost. We were a block away from the bench when the challenge was made. Not only was the penny at the bench, when we walked back, there were three pennies in a row on the same sidewalk we had just crossed. My son and his friend couldn't believe it and all they could do was smile. Now all of these people are finding coins and believing that God is real.

The point is not the coins, but the proof those coins couldn't have been in those places unless it was God. There are many stories surrounding these signs from God, too many to write about. God will use anything just to prove to us He's real. In the Bible there were the locusts, hail, frogs, etc., all signs from the same God back then who is still alive today. God will show Himself during challenges just to prove us right because of our belief. Using us to show them that He's real only gets them closer in developing a closer relationship with Him. We need to take on more challenges from others to get them to believe. Don't take on a challenge if you have any doubts because you'll only push the challenger further from God. Many people want to believe and are on the edge of believing because of unexplainable incidents, but they just need someone to prove what they really want to believe. God knows they're on the edge and that's why He sent them to you. He will never let us down because that one on the edge is too important to Him.

One dismal night I was sitting outside alone writing poetry describing my hurts and I started praying to God to send an angel to comfort me. I asked Him to allow the angel to hug me, letting me know that everything would be fine. I was in such a state of loneliness, I just felt that I was the only one in the world who was hurting like that. I felt everyone had turned their backs on me and nobody understood what I was going through.

First, I felt this calmness gather around my body that was indescribable. There was such a warmth that hugged me giving me an enormous peace as though to say, "I'm here and everything will be fine." A voice said, "Even though everybody else has turned their backs on you, I haven't." Then I felt like arms were wrapped around me as though it was my mom hugging me like when I was growing up. Immediately, I looked up to the sky and the clouds had formed three angels flowing by and later dissipated. I knew at that point, God had answered my prayer.

The next morning while on my walk, there were these white angel wings on the ground in front of me. They were like the ones kids would use for a Halloween costume, but it wasn't close to that holiday. Also, on my return walk, those same wings were on the other side of the alley in my walkway as though to say an angel was with me wherever I go. Someone would've had to move them. That didn't happen because there was nobody in the alley but me, yet it was God confirming everything was going to be fine.

Later that evening on another walk down the alley, those wings had disappeared. There are angels all around and watching out for us all the time.

One Sunday morning rushing to get dressed for church and not having cigarettes to smoke with my coffee, I needed to go to the store. The only money I had was the five-dollar bill and two ones that my ex-wife had given me the night before to give as an offering. I didn't want to use the money to buy the cigarettes, but later decided to only offer the amount left after buying the cigarettes. I got on the bike to save some time and rode to the corner store. When the cashier was waiting for the cigarette money, I reached into my pocket finding nothing; I had left the money at the house. So I left to go back to the house and on the way, there were six dollar bills on the ground in a straight line. I was happy and shocked at the same time because they weren't there when I was on my way to the store. I immediately turned around, went back to the store, bought the cigarettes, and went to the house to get ready for church.

There was no doubt in my mind that God made those bills appear. They weren't there when I went to the store or maybe I just didn't see them, but whichever way, God let me find them. I was riding to the store just as fast as I was returning back to get the money, so why didn't I see them? He knew it would've been wrong and I really didn't want to use the money given to me by my ex-wife for her offering. When she gave it to me, it was not mine to spend, yet it was

God's money. God knew this and that's why He made me leave it at the house the first time. Also, there was no way man would've lined those bills up like that, nor would they blow from the wind in a straight line if man just dropped them. He not only supplied my need, He gave me enough change so I could make my offering without having to touch any of the money my ex-wife gave me. When I got to church, I did give the money she gave me as her offering.

I was sitting on the patio one night having a cigarette fit, yet I had no money to buy a pack, nor did I want to ask my ex-wife for the money. I was talking to God and told Him I knew I needed to quit smoking, but I really needed a cigarette. Immediately after saying that, my stepdaughter opened the sliding door leading to the patio and handed me a handful of cigarettes. She said that her mother told her to give them to me.

Again, God allowed me to have the desire of my heart. He wanted me to know that He is a rewarder of those who diligently seek. There was no way my ex-wife knew that I was asking God for cigarettes and He used her to answer my prayer. As far as she knew, something just made her think of me needing cigarettes at that moment and she sent them out to me. I'm sure she didn't realize that it was God making her do this. The timing was perfect and it was God because man cannot read another man's mind. God will use our enemies if He has to in supplying our needs and desires.

I've found out that "rebuking the devil" really works.

There were many times my ex-wife would get home with her normal hangover and curse me out for something or another. Some of those times I just wasn't feeling it and instead of cursing back at her, I would quietly rebuke the devil in her. I knew it wasn't her, yet it was that bad spirit she was carrying around inside her. At first, I really didn't think I had the power to make the devil flee, but I soon realized I did.

One time I had gotten cursed out and instantly rebuked that devil, then went on doing what I was doing. A little later as I was sitting under the carport, my ex-wife had walked out to its gate with a plate of breakfast. She reached it over the gate to me and told me that I needed to eat and the plate of food was for me. I was shocked because she was just acting like the devil earlier and now like an angel.

There is no way that would've happened with my ex-wife if the rebuking didn't work. She was the type to allow her anger and cursing to linger throughout the day. It was unheard of especially in such a short time. Her attitude changed from night to day without an evening. We do have that power and the moment we notice the revelation of Satan, we need to rebuke that spirit and it has to leave. We also have to be careful of who we let into our homes because many bad spirits will come in if we invite them. Many times I rebuked and prayed with others who came in the name of the Lord and the existing problems went away. When two or more come in Jesus' name, there He also shall be. When God is involved, things have to change and Satan certainly doesn't like it. Satan would much rather we curse back and argue because then we give him all of the glory. The first thing ungodly man would've told me when she brought out the plate of breakfast was not to eat it for fear of poison or something. The same Jesus who rebuked those bad spirits out of men into those swine is the same Jesus who is alive today. We represent Him, come in His Name, know He lives in us, so why not rebuke bad spirits?

One day my ex-wife had cursed me out. She gave me a deadline to be out of her house, and made me so angry I had to go on a walk. I walked down the alley talking to God about the situation with my ex-wife and asking Him for help. As I walked across an intersection, there was this long-legged, bright-skinned, long-haired doll in the street. The doll was pulled apart with its parts in different places. I noticed it, yet still continued my walk to the corner store as normal, then back. During that period I couldn't get that torn-up doll out of my mind until I ran upon it on my way back to the house. I stopped and looked at the doll again and something told me not to worry about what my ex-wife was doing to me because sooner or later, she was going to be torn apart just like that doll. After accepting that, I went back to the carport and was at ease with the terrible situation. She knew that my son and I had nowhere to go but she wanted us out.

The doll was God's way of telling me to trust Him and

that she wasn't going to get away with those bad treatments. *Touch not my anointed or do my prophet no harm!* Her lifestyle was on a road of destruction and would end just like that doll (torn apart because of the streets). Each part of her life would be strung in different places with no place to go. When God shows you something and you cannot get it off of your mind, He's trying to tell you something. Lots of time we don't stop to listen. This doll described my ex-wife's physical appearance totally. What are the chances I would normally walk across a doll torn apart? There was no way man could've staged it that perfectly, nor would he have known the circumstances or reasons for my walk in the first place.

One night, I began to cry. It had gotten too much for me, especially not seeing any light, I thought, at the end. My son was asleep and I was glad so he wouldn't feel my excruciating pain. I got up, went outside to the carport, fell to my knees by this pole I anointed, and cried out to God. I had my forehead bowed onto the pole asking God for help, and I just couldn't stop crying. After I finished and pulled back from the pole, there were little bubbles of water up and down that pole. It wasn't condensation nor did I throw water on this pole. I was in shock and slowly moved back from it because that much was unbelievable. I stood back by the gate and watched those bubbles slowly disappear, but as they did, they formed into the shape of a heart. When I saw that happening, a peace came over me that was indescribable and all of my tears went away.

If someone would've told me this had happened and I didn't see it with my own eyes, I wouldn't have believed them. It was like God showed me He cried with me. The calmness and my dry tears told me that everything was going to be fine. The heart also told me that he felt the pain I was suffering inside of me. *A fervent prayer of a righteous man availeth much.* When Jesus asked God to take the cup away from Him, He knew that God's purpose had to be fulfilled no matter what. We have to stop asking God to take our cups away when things get hard and trust His will. He knows they are hard because He allowed them to happen to us only for His purpose. We appreciate all things more if we work hard for them rather than them being given to us. What we need to practice is telling God we know this situation is hard, but we accept it. After my experience, I was able to go back inside with a peaceful mind and go to sleep. It's not what goes in that defiles a man, yet what comes out (his heart)!

A little while after I started staying under the carport, I realized it was going to be a special place. One day a minister friend and I took our oil and anointed the circular area under the carport. We also anointed a small cross on both of the steel posts that were holding up the carport. Everything happened underneath the roof had to be sacred as a tribute to God because I knew He was there and that was my covering.

A few days later, I took a look at the oiled crosses. What I saw shocked me. The crosses had expanded to about double the original sizes, and there were halos around both crosses similar to Jesus' robes. At the bottom of each cross looked like there was a hill of dirt holding each cross, and you couldn't see the cross directly facing it, yet you could from side views. It was simply amazing. The thing that was so odd about the cross expansion was I could understand the oil flowing downward, but not outward in a straight line.

Everyone who saw those crosses was amazed, especially only being able to see them from side views. That carport was no doubt anointed by God because all of the people that passed had to look over to see what was going on. There were so many lost souls who seemed like they knew where to get prayer, conversation, greetings, hugs, or just a word from God. They would tell me that they didn't know why they walked that way but just did. You could feel the power of God under that roof and when you prayed under either of the crosses, it felt like the post would softly rock back and forth.

I went back to that carport months after leaving and those crosses were still there. When God stamps something, no one can remove it but Him and that includes our lives. When I would pray or just talk to someone there, you could feel God's holy presence and that's what made all of those people come back over and over.

One cloudy day I left out to go on my regular walk with God. All of the way until I got to the corner store, the sky just looked cloudy, yet there would be no rain. As I turned to leave the store, I looked up again at the sky and there were dark clouds. I prayed and asked God not to let it rain on me going back to the house because it was quite a way to go.

About a fourth of the way back, I noticed a shortcut back to the house which would've, I thought, missed the rain because I'd get back quicker. Just as I thought about taking it to make sure I didn't get rained on, something told me, "No, just walk your regular walk." I got all the way back in front of the carport without getting rained on and decided that I would walk a little further to the corner because I hadn't found any coins. Just as I passed the end of the carport, it started raining only on me. Everything around me had no rain and was dry. I couldn't believe what was happening to me, so I rushed underneath the carport and my personal shower stopped immediately.

This happened to me because God and I agreed on this certain path and that day I wanted to take a shortcut because of the strong possibility of rain. I focused on the clouds and not on my prayer to God. There is no shortcut in walking with God, nor any of His requirements. When we shortcut, that's when we get ourselves in lots of trouble causing our own pains and misfortunes. God never shortcuts with us, so why should we try it with Him? I was worried about the rain and possible storm on my long journey home, but I forgot about praying to God not to let it rain on me. When we walk with God, we are going to have storms in our lives, but we can't give up. Why didn't I truly believe in the One who controls the rain? Many times, even after God has kept His promise, we allow our fleshly thoughts to push things a little further. We're not satisfied only with the blessing He had just given us, yet we always want more. Also, it actually rained only on me and not my surroundings until I went under the carport.

Obedience is better than sacrifice! When we look at the clouds in our lives, we also misread them. Most times they are not as bad as they look, but we try to run for cover when really we didn't have to run at all, instead, just trust God. God is the only One who has the ultimate say in the storms of the sky and the storms of our lives. What would've happened if Abraham or Moses had been disobedient to God? People thought I was crazy when I told them about it raining only on me, but they thought that Noah was crazy too. We all know history showed who was crazy. We must always keep our eyes on God and not our surroundings because our surroundings will totally mess us up.

Many times, even at my old house, I would be sitting outside talking to God, staring forward, and I would see these clouds circling my entire body. At first it scared me but after getting used to it, I expected to see them. They would always flow upward and would continue for a while. They were like white cigarette smoke flowing when you hold a cigarette in front of your face. It echoed such a peaceful feeling. It also felt like your spirit was floating up to Heaven with your body still down on earth.

I was stunned the first time it happened and as of this writing, I am still stunned. I cannot explain it nor can I figure it out, but I do know it's an awesome feeling and a sign from God. It could be representing that God and I have such a personal relationship that He's showing me that I don't have to worry about the outside world. It also could signify that God is personally surrounding me because the Bible tells us God rode the clouds. I don't know what it is, but I know it gives me a protective feeling indicating that nothing can penetrate through.

Right before school began, I didn't have any money and my son didn't have any clothes to wear. He realized all of the other kids would have new clothes and he kept asking me when he was going to go shopping. I kept putting him off, but told him that it would happen. It had gotten to the last week before school started and we both were on edge. I got sad because I thought about making sure all the years my stepchildren had new school clothes and now I couldn't get the special son God blessed me with anything. I prayed and asked God to give me this son because I was jealous of my stepchildren's fathers having them with the woman I loved. I asked God to bless me with a son and God did just that. This was the one now I was unable to provide for, at least school clothes.

Suddenly a couple of days before school started, I spoke with my first ex-wife who sent me some money by her brother who was visiting with her. He and I set up a meeting place, met, and I picked up the money she had sent. Not only that, my ex-brother-in-law bought me some cigarettes because I was out, and gave us some extra money. The amount he gave me was more than the amount I needed to get my son's clothes. My son was able to wear his new clothes to school like the other kids. It also looked as if my ex-wife wasn't concerned, but I didn't let that bother me because I looked unto the Heaven.

Again, God had this thing already worked out even before I started to worry myself. Again, my ex-brother-in-law and first ex-wife were my rams in the bush. If we can ever trust God and believe He will supply all of our needs, we won't worry. If He gave me the son I described, why would I not think He'd take care of him, even when I couldn't?

F: THE CHURCH

A few days after moving into my ex-wife's house, I met this preacher who was living across the same street. The evening before, they had thrown a spiritual neighborhood block party and I watched it from a window inside of the house. We stood in front of the house and talked, then right before he left, he told me to think about being a deacon in his church. At that point, even though I knew God, I was scared of the responsibility and didn't really want to commit. He would invite me to weekly Bible study and Sunday service almost daily, but I kept putting him off. He told me during our first visit that he knew two powerful world renown preachers and he was their understudy. Sometime later, I decided since he knew these people, maybe they knew someone who would consider publishing my writings if they were good enough.

One day I took some of my best work and left it for him to review and to see if he thought it was good enough. Many days had passed and finally he came over and told me the writings were excellent and he kept copies to send to those powerful preachers. He also told me he wanted me to read one of the poems in his church service each Sunday if I decided to join. Just before he left, he told me he had just made up his mind that he was going ahead and put me on his church program because he knew I'd accept.

A few weeks passed and the pressure of unhappiness and the tension between my ex-wife and me was exploding, so I decided to take the preacher up on his invitation. At least I didn't have to be at the house for some hours of peace twice a week. So my son and I started going to both services. We could only wear the few clothes we had because all of our other clothes were still in storage. I couldn't go get any of them because we didn't have the space in the closet at the house nor would they allow me into the storage because I was behind on the payments. Shortly after we began, the preacher made me a deacon and my son an usher of his church and I began reading my poems each Sunday. The preacher even went out and bought my son a uniform to wear to church. The church would also serve a home-cooked meal each Sunday so my son and I wouldn't have to worry about eating at least on that day. The only thing that bothered me was not having offerings each time I went to the services. Sometimes we went to other church services and it embarrassed me because I wasn't able to put in an offering.

The one thing that I cherished was when we would go and have service at this nursing home. The elderly would remind me of my grandmother whom I loved very much and if I could say or sing something for them, it would give me great gratification. The longer we would stay all day on Sunday, the better because it took me away from the hell at home.

We need to be extremely careful about accepting positions in churches when we are immediately approached. Sometimes when this happens, the person in charge is only trying to fill seats, which is not ordained by God. Many times they tell you that God told them to give you that position, but you have to question whether God really said that, especially if they just met you. These people don't know anything about you, and putting you in charge of God's people is a mistake on their part, let alone if you do have a bad background. If they show any other motive toward you, there is a guarantee there are other motives not of God in their church. Beware if there is any doubt on your part and don't commit until you are sure or God tells you to. These people seems to love themselves more than God, and they have "I'm the boss" attitude.

They want others to look at them as God instead of acknowledging others' own personal relationships with God Himself. We forget many times that, no matter where we are or what we are doing, if we lift up God, then He'll draw people unto us. We won't have to go looking for them. When a church is having a tough time building a large congregation or holding onto the few they have, then there is a problem with something in that church. Someone isn't allowing God to use them and just playing with church because when God speaks, people listen. Look at the multitudes that followed Jesus and He didn't have to solicit them. His message went to a few who drew multitudes because His Word was real. When He healed all of those people, they had to tell others who had to draw near Him. If God's Word goes out, it won't come back void. There's too many church people playing church and in the process losing the lost or confusing their minds. How can you serve God at a church and Satan the same day at home? You cannot serve two masters and a house divided cannot stand. Here's a simple way to tell whether a church is of God or not. After the visit, if you don't remember something out of the mouth of the preacher that hit you personally and made you want to return, then something's wrong. You can count on there being a hidden fleshly agenda somewhere. If God told you to do something in His name, then He will have everything you need to be successful, especially the people.

We also find ourselves not going to church because

we're worried about our clothes. It is not your outward appearance that God is concerned with, it's your inside appearance. When you die, you won't need those clothes anyway, you can't take them with you to either place. I'd rather be badly dressed, pure of heart, and going to heaven rather than a "sharp dresser" going to hell. Keeping up with the Joneses doesn't get you to heaven because those are only material things they put before God anyway. Would you rather be a "richer than rich" person worried how to keep your riches, or would you rather allow God to supply all of your needs and be at peace each day?

Initially we did go just to get away from our problems, but as the weeks passed, something changed inside of me. It wasn't me escaping to the church or any of that, rather it was rounding out my one-on-one with God. This was a personal thing that ventured over to my son getting closer to God in his limited understanding. He would be taking a shower and I would hear him singing one of the church songs or he'd read the Bible asking lots of questions. I realized later that he was just trying to sing away the hurt he was experiencing for the lack of a real mother.

There was this one elderly woman at the nursing home that really took me back reminding me so much of my grandmother. We must never say never of what we can do when it comes to truly doing God's work from our hearts. One Sunday evening at the home, I was asked to sing a solo, which I had never done, and I started singing "I Am

Redeemed." God gave me notes I had never known to exist and "tore the house down." Almost everyone in the room began to cry, including me. The little old lady cried like a baby that day, but a few months passed and I never saw her again. Although when we got back, and the home problems were still there, I had the strength to bear them. God gave me the strength, wisdom, patience, and everything I needed to deal with the problems. I refused to let the devil win. I lived by "greater is He that's in me, than he that's in the world."

G: CHURCH FAMILY

This church was a family type operation with a dictator mentality. What they wanted or said was how it went and there was no debate allowed. They exhibited a "more holier than thou" attitude which drove a lot of possible members away. Their "in charge" behavior caused fear among the weak. They would brag about the ones who were able to give, in an open forum, making the less fortunate feel even less. They completely misinterpreted the word "submission" because they thought it meant "slavery" unto them. There were many deacons and ministers placed in the positions for reasons of need, rather than allowing God to promote them to lead His people. Of course, we would see them a couple of Sundays and we'd never see them again. That was the same with the congregation; they would visit a time or two, then they never would return. This happened to some of the members of my own family and friends. They said something about the services didn't feel right and made them not want to return. There were complete family members who supported the church for months consistently, yet they just up and left because of the upper management problems. The upper management was manipulating each other for power and that demeanor echoed negatively down to the few church members. When they talked to their members and potential members, their "much holier than you" tone drove people away. They would chastise their workers in public if things didn't go just the way they expected. They made you feel that God and you didn't have a connection or relationship, yet God has to tell them to tell you something. When we would go to gatherings, they expected a special treatment to boost their personal egos. Most of the time, they were treated like common folk and deemed them no special attention at all.

Most of the family members held positions in the church. When any of them would get upset, for whatever personal or church reason, they just wouldn't show up, leaving that position open. The other faithful members would step in and cover those openings, yet when the family members would get over whatever, they would get reinstated pushing the faithful members back aside. This practice wasn't fair to those faithful members and most of them left the church because of the selfish practices. They would always brag about how much of their own money they were putting into the church, but they forgot that they were the ones trying to build a church. Also, it was nobody's problem but theirs if they couldn't realize there's a problem inside the church discouraging increased membership. Ex-members all echoed that there was something wrong in the atmosphere of the church that was uninviting.

Upper management of a church must realize there are too many other churches around and people have a choice. We also must realize that the people trying your church are sent by God and He will see how you treat his lambs. If your agenda is not of or from God, He will remove them from your hands. Why would God allow you to hurt the already hurt? Family operations will only succeed if all of the members are on the same page. Jealousy with suspicious behavior will normally occur, which will bring division in the most important part of the operation, getting souls to Jesus. Even though you try hard to completely separate family and church, it is almost impossible to achieve, especially in making decisions. Conning and discipleship are two different definitions when it comes to the realness of God. Conning the lost only gets them through the door if your game was good, yet most of the time they still don't come. If they do come, they will soon realize that your motive was wrong and they won't return. If we truly lift up Jesus, they and more will be drawn to the Jesus who lives in you. Most people will recognize a falseness from the start, simply because they have been hurt by false before. Jesus didn't have to perpetrate to get the multitudes to follow Him. There is only one God and man cannot be Him.

We have too many upper management representatives of churches who place themselves at the level of God. The reason they cannot fill their empty chairs is because they are not Jesus-like. They say that Jesus lives in them and that Jesus, through them, is preaching, but where is the fruit? Good trees produce good fruit and good trees cannot produce bad fruit. Where are the waiting multitudes to fill those empty seats if you're speaking for Jesus and why are your words coming back void? God is the Word and when His Word goes out, it doesn't come back void, so whose words are you speaking? Quoting scriptures by memorizing does not impress God, but your positive actions and the love in your heart does. You may fool the less informed and weaker lambs for a while, but God will expose your realness, if your motives aren't right. You don't have to brag boldly to convince others that Jesus lives in you. That light will shine on its own and draw them to you without you even saying a word. It may be your smile, greeting, demeanor, wave, laughter, eye contact, or something that makes a person notice that there's something very special and different about you. When they see the realness, they will want to be around you all of the time. Most of those who have to validate their perpetration, normally will have ungodly motives they're trying to hide. Any time you get mad because you're not the center of attention, you allow your pride to take over. If you're truly allowing God to order your footsteps, then you won't get prideful and mad at God. You are placing the behavior of man higher than the behavior of God and excluding who loves you more. If God wanted you to be that center of attention, He would have made it happen. Preachers or any other church management cannot put you on their backs and carry you to heaven with them. You have to have a one-on-one personal relationship with Jesus. God doesn't love the preacher or the others no more than He loves you. preachers are not God, nor are they on the same level as God! All they can do is deliver His Words and tell you how to get to know Him. How can you replace a lost lamb with a wolf in sheep's clothing and expect it to last? The wolf will run the other sheep away trying to destroy them. Why would you even put him in the same pasture?

You can put all the money in the world into a church, but if it's not of God, sooner or later it will fall. Bragging about your deed won't change the fall. Never brag about your much around others of less.

Jesus showed His greatness by His doings. When His mother and brothers tried to speak to him when He was with the multitudes, He didn't give them special treatment, yet included them with all of the other brothers and sisters. What if Jesus would've looked down upon (degraded) all of those people He healed like the blind men, the old woman with the blood disease, the leper, etc., and still expected them to follow Him? Church management just doesn't get it because it's not supposed to be about them. They're only supposed to be God's vessels. Jesus told Peter upon this rock I will build my church and the gates of hell shall not prevail against it. So, if most churches state that their church is built of God and it's God's house, then why is there so much hell inside their walls?

H: THE PREACHER

When I worked in the corporate world, God blessed me with skills which prepared me for His plan. I think the preacher saw those skills in me and instead of allowing me to structure his church, I felt he thought I wanted to take it over. He wanted to use my skills to get credit for himself, yet only the ones that boosted his ego. He had no experience, yet disregarded that there was a business side also to building a church. When I would try to implement these beginnings, he would make me feel like I was getting too aggressive and personal into his dealings. His ignorance in business and personality showed, yet he was too "high and mighty" to face his imperfections. I also sensed an act of jealousy, especially when lost souls would ask me to pray for them, people would gather around me instead of him, and people would call me on the phone for counsel instead of him. I would gather them up each Sunday morning, load them in my car, and we would go to church. I know he looked upon them as being beneath him but he tolerated them because he needed them as a member count in his church. He would always judge and negatively talk about their downfalls, yet their money and food were good enough for him to accept. He would always brag about this young minister he was totally using for money and making the people I brought feel bad or unimportant. There were many times I wouldn't have enough gas to get to and from church, yet God always made a way. Many times the preacher would ask me to pick up people that were closer to him without providing me gas for my car. He knew I didn't have the money, yet I felt he was trying to pay me back for the times he gave me a ride to church. Again, he was the one trying to build a church and using my skills to help build it without payment.

I remember picking up one deacon almost every Thursday and Sunday. He lived ten miles out of my way, not counting the miles to and from the church house, taking him to Bible study and church. He never gave me gas money for doing that. I strongly felt that he was using me, but God always provided enough gas to get us there and back. Many times I prayed to God to let us make it back home because I was driving on gas fumes and He did. The thing that bothered me the most was his frequent and daily visitation. It had gotten to the point, I used to hate to see him walk or drive up. He would ask me to ride with him to a specific place, yet we would ride all over, with him being inconsiderate of my time and obligations. This would become a daily occurrence almost giving me no time for my own obligations. He would come to my house early, sit all day, gossip about the neighborhood, walk when I didn't want to walk, read when I didn't feel like reading, disciple when I wasn't ready to disciple. These last-minute and demanding tactics would also occur with my extreme and many responsibilities in the church. He would literally get upset when I wasn't able to lead songs if my voice had problems. He would get on me for smoking cigarettes, yet when he'd have personal problems at home, he would come over to my house and smoke cigarettes. He would preach on other marriage failures while his marriage was falling apart. He had personal motives for attracting young females to the church. His lust for one of them almost got him in trouble. He was definitely a preacher with his own agenda, not God's.

One time there was this kid killed in the same alley I used to walk in. Instead of going on over to the scene to see if he could help the family in their sorrow, he decided to go to his house and change clothes because he knew the media was interviewing people. He finally made it to the scene and was ignored by the family when he told them he was a preacher. His presentation certainly echoed his ego, especially when he invited the media to him before talking to the family. He found one family member to talk to, yet when they agreed to interview with the media, the family was the main ones the media wanted to talk to. Finally he got his opportunity and he began talking about the system failing the young man who was killed, not knowing any background on this kid. He and this other family member set up a meeting with this funeral home. The state was going to pay for the entire funeral and probably pay the preacher for his message. Somehow I felt his motives were wrong and he was so involved because of money or prestige or maybe both.

After all of that, the family secretly stopped all of the arrangements he had set up, had another funeral director pull the body from the other home, and have the funeral somewhere else. When the guy from the first funeral home called him telling him the family had just pulled the body, he was devastated. He tried not to let it show, but it was obvious. His beginning motives were wrong and that's why things went the way they did at the end. If his help motive had been sincere, none of this ever would've happened.

God will put people in our lives with voids we lack to help us complete His plan. The only way it doesn't work is if man is making his/her own plan creating confusion and not fully utilizing the tools God gave him/her. When we place ourselves above needing help from others, we may be turning our backs on ones God sent to us. God knows where we are weak even if we don't acknowledge our weaknesses, and sends others to make us strong in those areas. He gives us a choice to use them or not to, believing our way is better than His way.

Satan will confuse our minds. All through the Bible,

God put people together to fill in the other one's weaknesses. Unlike us, they acknowledged their weakness and accepted the one God sent so God's purpose could be fulfilled. Using people or their assets for a personal motive is not of God and will soon come to an end, especially when the one using is claiming to do things in God's name. When you use lost lambs for your own benefit or satisfaction, God isn't happy because He sent them to you for a specific purpose of establishing a relationship with Him. *Woe unto the shepherd who scatters my sheep!*

Every time I would be low on gas, God would send me someone who would bless me with gas or the money to buy the gas. Although I was being used, God knew and would never leave or forsake me because I wasn't doing it for man. Instead of the preacher hanging with me, I felt that he should've been training his young ministers, visiting the sick, working with the homeless, counseling the lost, recruiting others lost in the streets, etc. He should've realized something was wrong. I should've realized from the start when I was lied to about my writings, that something was wrong. I feel I had to go through all of this experience so next time, I would know the difference in preachers much earlier. This also taught me that there are preachers who are wolves in sheep's clothing. They just cover themselves with the wool a little better than most. We cannot force our religion on anyone, we can only offer a chance to know Jesus. They have the choice to accept or reject our offer and then it's between them and God.

Preachers need to clean up their own house before preaching and counseling to others with the same kind of dirt. Many preachers and church folks alter the Word just to fit their own shortcomings, yet no alteration is designed for others. The Bible teaches us not to add to nor take away from the Word, so who gives them that authority? Criticism of others only becomes weight if we are critical of ourselves. We must learn that there are no double standards in God. Our outside coverings, no matter how good, don't hide our thoughtless hearts. Personal gratification, exposure, gain, or motives used in helping the lost souls always backfire on us.

I: LEAVING THE CHURCH

There was too much ungodliness, disorganization, personal/business problems, and selfishness that made me quit. I could no longer ask people to follow this church because it was the preacher's church and not God's. I didn't tell my previous followers to stop going, yet left that choice up to them. There was only one member who kept going, but a few weeks after, even she quit. She couldn't take the preacher's constant demand to go to church every Sunday even when she didn't feel good, calling late at night at her home. I knew the exact day when it was time for me to leave because God gave me the signs early one Sunday morning.

The preacher talked about most of the ones that

followed me to his church in a negative way many times. That only showed me that he wanted them to attend his church only for numbers and their money. One of those members asked him many times to come to her house to bless it, but he just kept promising her and never did. That was wrong because he made it a point to bless others' homes without hesitation. He was only cordial with her because he wanted to date one of the women she knew. He tried to con her out of her car to no avail, but he did con her out of four or five nice chairs for the church. He refused to bless her house saying it was too nasty, yet he accepted the chairs from inside of that nasty house. She gave him the chairs out of love. She said one time he saw her in a grocery store and very loudly asked her to let him buy some food stamps from her. Why did he embarrass her that way? This was after she also stopped going to his church and I guess he was trying to pay her back by degrading her.

At this point, he didn't care if she came back or not because of her outspoken behavior, especially after she told him about her problem with him trying to sleep with the woman she introduced to his church. He would stay on my couch and call this same woman on his cell phone trying to get with her. After I stopped going, he decided to ask me to pay back the money he had loaned me to pay for my apartment deposit and get my stuff out of storage. He never mentioned it until I stopped going to his church and refused to be his buddy anymore. One thing he forgot was all of the furniture I gave him when I removed it out of storage, including two Queen Anne chairs I had given to the church but went to his house. He also forgot the day he was excited when we agreed to pay back the storage loan in groceries which I did. So to get him from coming around, I paid him the last fifty dollars for that deposit in three trips. The worth of all of the furniture I had given him certainly surpassed the amount of money I owed or he thought I owed. All that did was show his greed. I also could've charged for all of the services I did for him. *Touch not my anointed or do my prophet no harm!* If we go to a church and feel something isn't right, chances are it's God telling us it isn't. If He does show you, then you need to find a righteous church to worship and leave that one. Don't stay for the sake of position, long-time membership, fear, or any other fleshly reasons. Trust me, it won't get better. Satan finds weaknesses in churches and welcomes himself in also. Lost lambs follow good shepherds and they can sense when there is rough water they are being led into. There are too many people who have already been hurt by churches and scared to try others; we have to exhibit realness. We cannot have it both ways, nor can we show love toward all differently. God will give us signs for exiting a house that is supposed to be built in His Name because we are too important to Him to hurt. Are there any real houses of God where the sick can go for real and legitimate healing? Most of the lost souls have tried some churches, finding out most of them are all the same. All they are interested in is money, fame, etc., instead of getting one single hurting soul to know Jesus. They don't understand that the one soul saved is their multitude because that saved soul will disciple another, who will disciple another, and it just goes on and on. We don't need to worry about getting large numbers, yet focus on one at a time. When a church continues to have a rotating door, something is wrong and the management needs to look objectively, then the problem will jump out at them. The biggest decision they will face is correcting the problem because they will find it at the top end of management. They will find out that God is missing from the agenda. If we know one of our followers or members has a house that's nasty, then we as the children of God should do all in our powers to help them clean it up, that is instead of degrading them. Money is the root of all evil and that's what happens when people don't get their ways. You are the greatest thing that ever lived when you're helping others. But as soon as you stop being used and make a stand, all of a sudden those financial gifts that were "given" to you quickly become loans. Then, there is this thing called memory loss. We are bound by God's law to love and forgive, but there's nothing requiring us to stay in their presence.

CHAPTER EIGHT

AGAINST THE ODDS OF SATAN

A: EXITING DEVIL'S DEN

One day my stepdaughter asked me if I wanted to go with her to apply for a low-income apartment. She said she had already put in her application and she was going over to check on her status. I believe the real truth was she was told by my ex-wife to find a ride and take me over there so I could leave her house. That didn't matter because I truly wanted to get out anyway. So I went with her and put in my application with the apartment manager informing me it would probably take about two months for a vacancy to surface. Even though it seemed too long, at least there seemed to be a light at the end of a tunnel. People told me that this apartment complex had a reputation of bad and deadly incidents, but that still didn't bother me.

Just because my son and I only had a few more months to live with my ex-wife, it didn't change any of the abusive treatment we were getting. So many days and nights I prayed for God to rush the process so my son and I could finally have our own home with some peace of mind.

About a month and a half later, I finally got the call from the complex that my name came up for an apartment. They wanted me to come in and complete the paperwork. My ex-wife's boyfriend John drove me over there. When I first saw the complex, it was evident how people had described the place. There was lots of truth to it. I told John that I hoped they would assign me an apartment on the front street next to the office. I felt at least we would have a better chance of being safe.

On my walks with God in the alley, He had placed keys in my walkway letting me know He was going to open up some doors for me. Afterward, I felt a little better because I knew He was setting up our new home and it wouldn't be long. There were many other times during walks I felt that I couldn't wait but He reminded me just to trust Him. God knew where He was going to send me and used my stepdaughter as a guide. Many times we don't understand why we're guided in a certain direction, but only God can see our future. A lot of times God sends us to places we may not like or certainly we wouldn't have chosen, but He knows what's best for us. One thing we have to come to grips with, we cannot rush God because our time is not His time. He lets us know through signs and tells us what the signs mean. It is up to us to believe or disbelieve what our heart is telling us.

B: OLD BAGGAGE WITH STEPDAUGHTER

A few weeks later, the apartment complex called my stepdaughter, gave her an apartment, and she packed up and left. She was extremely happy because she didn't have to take her mother's abuse anymore. I had to walk the alley and talk to God about the jealousy I was feeling because she was blessed and I wasn't. After my stepdaughter and her kids left, my ex-wife stepped up her sarcasm concerning my son and me. She would comment that she couldn't wait until she had her house to herself, still asking me why my son and I didn't want to go live with my relatives.

She would constantly ask about the date we thought we were going to leave. She'd ask if I called the apartment complex about my status. One week before Thanksgiving, my daughter was over for a visit and we began to talk about my situation of abuse. She told me that my son and I could come and stay with her and her boyfriend until my apartment was ready. One day my ex-wife got so nasty, I called my stepdaughter, asked her to come pick us up, and packed up the things we would need. She came over one night, we loaded her car, and went over to her apartment. We stayed there for a week, but I didn't feel as invited as I thought we'd be. We had to sleep on her sofa with our belongings still in our suitcases, which was no change from her mom's house. They closed their bedroom door most of the times, which was the only bathroom entrance, making us have to go outside when we had to go. I would be asked to babysit my grandkids all of the time. I felt I had to because we were living there. I would walk to the complex office every day to check on my status. My stepdaughter soon made me feel like we were intruding on her privacy and she didn't want us there anymore. Again, I found a route to walk with God to pray about my situation because I felt I moved from one hell to another. The signs of the pennies continued and again I would stay outside most of the days into the nights.

One day my son and I went over to the office and the manager finally told me she had assigned us an apartment but we'd have to wait until they fixed it up. She said it probably would take about a week to get it done which made me happy and sad at the same time. I was happy because I knew then we would have our own place and sad that we had to continue living as we were. The manager told us which one she assigned us and my son and I walked over to see it. When we got there, I was greatly disappointed because all of my furniture wouldn't fit because it was an efficiency, instead of a one-bedroom. Also, it was sitting in a bad position in the complex that made me feel very unsafe. Even though I wasn't happy, I was going to accept it just to get away from the intrusion I was feeling.

I went back to my stepdaughter's apartment finding pennies as I told God of my unhappiness, and continued to pray about that situation. I sat there for a while and God told me to go back to the office and ask the manager if she had an empty one-bedroom. The first time I went being obedient, the apartment office was closed. Again, my son and I went back over to the assigned one and looked inside, but didn't feel any better after we left. I went to the office another couple of times and on the third round, the manager was there. I went in. At this point I didn't want to hound her because I didn't want her to take it from me and put my name back on the list. So I accepted thinking God told me to come and just as I began to walk out the door to leave, she said to wait and let her look at something. She looked in this black binder and saw this name still listed on a one-bedroom apartment that should've been gone. She verified that the occupant had left and told me that if I wanted that one, she'd give it to me but she wasn't supposed to do it. I asked her where it was and she pointed straight across the lot next to the office and told me it was the corner apartment. With no hesitation, I told her to write my name in that spot. Immediately, my son and I went over to the apartment, peeped through the windows, and found it to be perfect. It was just big enough to fit all of my furniture, on the same street I wanted, and close to the office for security. One more interesting point was it was apartment number 304, which was the same number on the house I grew up in with my mom and grandmother. I was so overwhelmed with joy, I just began to thank God over and over.

I left the apartment and went back over to the office and

thanked the manager again. She said it would be ready for us to move in about two weeks from then. I felt a little more relief and asked God to give me strength to bear the abuse for at least two more weeks.

The following day was Thanksgiving and I helped my stepdaughter prepare the meal because her mom was going to stop by. When my ex-wife and her friend came by, they ate and left. Before leaving, she invited my son and me back over to her house until my apartment was ready. I was hesitant but realized either place was just as bad. I made up my mind that same night that I would take her up on her offer after I got stuck babysitting for a long time that same night.

Everyone is looking out for themselves and forgetting to love thy neighbor as thyself. Most times they will ask you to do things they wouldn't normally ask of you because they know you have no choice. They take advantage of your terrible situation for their own selfishness. No matter where you go, take God with you. Walk with Him in your good or better times as you did in your bad times. God showed me with the pennies that He was still with me at my stepdaughter's home as He was at my ex-wife's home. Instead of people being up-front letting you know you're not welcomed, they take the cowardly way out throwing hints over and over. They don't realize that one day they may be in the same position needing someone like you and chances are God will put them there.

When I was about to give up on the efficiency apartment

they assigned us, even though I didn't want it, I was going to accept what God had for us. What I had forgotten was my prayer for a one-bedroom on the front street and by the office. We forget or give up on our desires from God, but isn't it good that God doesn't? He knew I was going to ask that prayer when I first went to the apartment, so He held that name on the list in that binder until I came. He waited until I had given up and was about to walk out of the office, then he showed me that "ram in the bush."

God does things in this fashion because He wants to show us there is no other explanation except Him. I'm sure my stepdaughter was pressured by her boyfriend for us to leave because of their lack of complete privacy. He wasn't supposed to be living there anyway, but family hardly ever comes first this day and time. *Touch not my anointed and do my prophet no harm* was unknown because of the devilish spirits in that apartment. It shocked me when my ex-wife invited us back to her house. It wasn't her, yet it had to happen to fit in God's plan. Many times people are with you while you are suffering, but as soon as they do better, they forget about you. But, aren't we glad God will never leave us or forsake us and will be close until the end? We forget God blesses us to bless others.

C: JOHN'S DEATH

After church the following Sunday, I asked the preacher

to drop me at my ex-wife's house since he just lived across the street from her. This time around, it was not as bad as the first time staying there. The mood was up and down and one day when it was good, she came out to the carport and gave me a study Bible. After just a week, the manager called me to come get my key and I could move in whenever I wanted to. My ex-wife's other friend John took me over there. I picked up the keys, checked the apartment out, and he drove me back. I was extremely happy because now my son and I had our own place and it wouldn't cost me a red penny. I was going to move out that following weekend but I had no money and even after saving it before them auctioning it off the first time, my time was due again the next second weekend. I couldn't find the money anywhere so something told me to call my same friend who lived out of town for help. When I called, she told me not to worry, but she couldn't come down until the following week. I accepted that because that was all I knew to do because I had no money or truck.

One day my ex-wife got me so upset, I called the preacher and asked him if he could drop me off at my apartment. I told him that I was fed up and I just couldn't take more. He dropped me off and told me that he would come back through after he handled his business. I went back, continued to rebuke the devil, and tried to stay away from her. It was real cold, but again I would spend mostly all of my time outside under the carport and walking the alley.

That Thursday, John, preacher, and I were in the alley and we invited John to go to church the following Sunday. John refused stating that he had some work to do and he had to make that money. We told him that tomorrow wasn't promised to him, that he needed to get himself right. We went on and John didn't go to church that Sunday with us. John came back over Monday night while I was watching the football game and was in a very playful mood with the kids and myself. Then we sat down at the table and he told me he had some allotments going into an account in another state. He said that he was going to find out how much he had in there and was going to pull enough out the next day to help my ex-wife catch up on all of her bills. He told me how much he loved her and wished that she would love him back, and leave all of those other guys alone. I told him I felt that he was the best man for her and her children.

He got up, went to her bedroom, lay beside her, and went to sleep in her bed. Around 1 a.m. to 2 a.m. while my son and I were asleep on the mattress, I woke up to my wife screaming for me to come to her bedroom because something was wrong with John. I got up, rushed into her room, and found John kneeling on the floor opposite from where she was sitting in the bed. I wrapped my two arms under his arms, picked him up, and put him back on the bed. I called out his name but he didn't respond.

I told my ex-wife to call 911. The operator told us to put him on his side. At first I thought he was having convulsions, but he wasn't acting with the same symptoms my brother had when he would have them. The next thing I heard was two or three moans, then silence. I felt for a pulse, but I didn't find one and I knew John had died but I didn't let the family know he was gone. The paramedics came, picked him up, and took John to the hospital, where later he was pronounced dead.

My ex-wife and kids were devastated over his death and mourned several days. She said she needed to change that bedroom around, but I told her it wouldn't matter because she couldn't change what had happened. It's funny about fleshly personal gifts because as long as you are submissive, it is no debt. As soon as debtor's luck changes and the money is short or you distance yourself a little, the gift becomes a debt. I had also given up the first time on my storage, but God's grace was sufficient. Not only did He provide the money to catch up, He blessed me with enough to pay for the exact time needed until I moved into the apartment. I didn't know but God knew all of the time how much time I needed.

How many times do your choices promise you help and at the last minute, something always comes up where they can't help? When God picks the person, He knows the promise will be totally completed with everything you need. He already has it planned out even before it happens.

With John, God didn't want him to withdraw that money because it would've been too easy for my ex-wife, especially the way she treated him. He loved her, yet she just used him instead of being grateful for his love. I knew then why God had me accept my ex-wife's invitation to return to her home. I needed to be there for her and the kids when John died in her bed. Even though she treated me terribly, she needed me to comfort her during his death. That's the reason you try so hard to help people and treat them the way you would want to be treated because you may have to go back to those same ones you mistreated for help. When she wanted to turn her bedroom furniture around, I told her if she put the furniture on the ceiling, nothing would change. I told her that was a true sign from God telling her she needed to get herself right because she could see how close she came to death. The death angel came in, looked at both of them in bed, and took John because and only because she was being prayed for. I told her it could've taken them both, but God either had mercy on her giving her another chance or He still had plans for her. Either way, she needed to get closer to Him. I had to be there to give her that message. I just hope that when I went into the room and found John on his knees that he was repenting to God. Accepting our invitation for church wouldn't have saved him, yet if he would've gone and accepted Jesus into his life, then he would've been fine. I just hope within those days, he got ready. All of our steps are ordered by God whether we know it or not.

D: NEW BEGINNING WITH SATAN WAITING

The only day my out-of-town friend could come was the day I had to have all of my furniture out of the storage room or the next day they would auction it off. That day came, she had some problems come up at work, and it looked like she wouldn't be able to come. The more the day went by, the more nervous I got, but either way I was going to move into my apartment with or without furniture. I didn't want to lose the clothes I needed for church and my son's other clothes. The moment I gave up and accepted the fact that I'd lost all of my stuff, my friend called. She told me she was on her way and was almost where I was staying. I still was scared because I really didn't think we had enough time before the store closed. She finally made it, picked my son and me up, and made it in time to rent a truck which she paid for and we got to the storage store before they closed. We loaded the truck, then ran into the problem of not being able to get the truck back in time before additional charges were added. We emptied the storage room with one truck trip and what a blessed feeling that was. Not only did she help me load the truck, but she also helped me unload it at my apartment. I forgot that her ex-husband supervised this same storage company in and around Texas, so she called him explaining our situation and he called and approved the truck return without additional payment.

We finally finished, returned the truck, and on the way

back she bought us something to eat. The following week, I stayed in my apartment by myself thanking God and putting everything in its place. I left my son with his mother so he could finish his last week in school. When I finished setting the apartment up, it was the exact amount of furniture we needed to fill each room. It was beautiful after I finished and I would stand back, look at each room, and thank God. My son couldn't wait until I went back to his mother's house to pick him up. When my son came, he was just like a brand-new kid. We had our own place and nobody could tell us how to live, how much to eat, how many showers to take, when we could iron our clothes, etc. My son was like a child with a new toy.

Even though you try hard to trust and believe in God, Satan knows your weakness in belief and will cause you to worry without need. He will make you give up and accept the worst. Really, when we give up on our prayers, we give up on God's promise. Unlike man, when God places His hand on a happening, you can count on it without any doubts. He'll open every door that Satan will try to close in the path. That's where Satan had me an hour before the storage store closed. When God comes through on one thing, we think that Satan is through with us, yet it's the opposite. He tries harder to get to us because he just wants us to give him a little opening and that's all he needs to come through. God set up the time with each plan even if we can't see it at the time. God knew what size truck we needed for the furniture. God had all of these plans scheduled to the very detail. Why won't we trust Him enough and keep our sanity? That's why He made me call that friend because He knew her ex-husband could authorize the extra time. Any other friend wouldn't have had the pull that my friend's husband had.

Nothing is impossible when comes to God! A real friend will come through for you without any strings attached, yet a pure heart. These friends don't forget about the times many have helped them in their times of need. My friend worked all day long, drove about a hundred miles, then helped me load and unload the truck. She did all of this and still had a smile on her face after we finished, a real friend. God also heard my son's cries of mistreatment like the Israelites and parted the Red Sea so we could walk through. We both went to a better place on the other side that God had prepared for us. God knew that his little heart didn't need to hurt anymore, even though his hurt came from his mother.

E: EX-WIFE'S DOWNFALL

About two weeks later, my ex-wife's electricity got turned off and her landlord told her she was losing the house for non-payment of rent. It made me wonder why her men friends didn't come through for her. I was gone and they had two weeks to catch up if they really cared about her knowing that I wouldn't be there to use it. It had gotten cold and without electricity, that meant they didn't have hot water. They couldn't cook meals, couldn't take hot showers, and had no heat to stay warm. These conditions went on for months until finally it got too much for her to bear. She was forced to put all of her stuff in storage and move with my older stepdaughter. Living in a one-bedroom apartment were my older stepdaughter, her boyfriend, my younger stepdaughter, my two grandchildren, and my ex-wife. My ex-wife and my younger stepdaughter had to sleep on the sofa together kind of like we had to do on the mattress. She had to wash their clothes at a wash-a-teria. I'm sure there were shower and bath issues since there were so many in the house with only one bathroom, which limited her. There was also a food problem because my older stepdaughter didn't follow up on her food stamps, so the state stopped them. Also, if my ex-wife's men friends cared that much for her, why didn't they get her and my younger stepdaughter a place to live?

This went on for a while and there was no calm, happiness, or peace in that apartment. It had gotten so bad that my ex-wife would stay with one of her girlfriends or one of her men friends for days trying to find peace, but found there was none. She decided to put in an application for her own low-income apartment on the same property as my stepdaughter and me. Her world had fallen apart in front of her eyes and she tried to ease the pain through continuing to serve Satan, even finding out that wasn't working for her. Every place she went, she had no place to go. One day she came to my apartment, knocked on the door, and asked me if she could come in and just lie down for a while. I told her to come on in, lie down in my bed, and rest as long as she wanted to. She also asked me if she could take a shower and I told her she could take as many as she wanted. She asked me for coffee and I told her I would make a fresh pot of coffee for her. She would borrow food when they were out and I opened up the refrigerator and cabinets for her to take whatever she wanted. She asked me to borrow quarters so she could do their washing and I gave her what she needed or what I had. Then she cried and told me that she knew how I felt when I stayed with her. She knew how it felt not having anywhere to go and just walking through an endless dark tunnel with no end in sight. I told her to sit down in the same chair she used to curse me out in and I prayed for her. Then I walked my entire route with God and cried, asking God to please bless her with her own home and to make them rush giving her the apartment. Each time I would ask on that walk, God would show me a penny and from that time, I knew God was going to help her. I even talked to the property management on her behalf and a few weeks later, they gave her an apartment.

I told her then she needed to thank and praise God for that blessing and that she needed to go to church with me one Sunday. She did that one Sunday and then stopped. Not only did she stop, when things started getting better for her, she went back to her old demons. Satan was just waiting for her to forget what God had done for her. At that point, Satan knew that she wasn't strong enough and all he had to do was tempt her with all of the ungodly things she liked. You cannot do God's people any kind of way and allow Satan to deceive you into thinking you'll get away with it. Sooner or later God will bring you down just to remind you what you did and most likely, put you in that same position you placed others in. Your friends will tell you anything while you all are feeling you're doing good, but as soon as you drop to ground zero, they're nowhere to be found. Satan will always let you find out the hard way; he's not your friend unless you're serving him. God is your friend and even when you're in the midst of Satan, He's always there. Also, be careful what you say you'll never do.

My younger stepdaughter would always say that she'd never live on the property where I got my apartment because it was too ghetto. She had to eat her words when she had to move there because she had nowhere else to go. Never say never because you don't know what God has planned for you. God put all of those who were so nasty to my son and me in the same house knowing that they couldn't help but get on each other's nerves. God took care of my son and me because He waited just until we left to turn off the electricity. It wasn't paid while we were there so it should've already been turned off. God is true to his signs and words because when he showed me the broken doll in the middle of the street, it came to reality.

One thing we have to be careful about, when God sends

those ones who did us wrong back to us, we have to forgive them and show them nothing but love. He'll most likely place them in a position to need what they didn't help you with. Open your arms and welcome them in and do not do to them what they did to you. It's hard and your pride will try to get in the way, but you have to put those feelings aside because, if not, you'll be the same as them. They will be greatly surprised because they're expecting you to turn your back on them, but you don't because God has never turned His back on us. When God cleans up our mess and we decide to go back to that same mess, then our next messy fall is going to be much worse than the one He cleaned up at first. He brings us out to give Him all of the praise and to help someone He sends our way to prove He can do it and the only One who can do it. Why is it that when we get better, we tend to turn back to Satan instead of going forward with God?

F: STEPDAUGHTER'S FALL

My stepdaughter had her apartment back to herself, her kids, and her boyfriend and thought her world was where she wanted it to be. She had transportation from her boyfriend and she could go where she wanted to go. God had also blessed her with an income tax refund of $2,500. I was on a walk with God when I heard she got it and was a little jealous because I had only received $77 on my refund. It bothered me because I was trying to walk with Him and she wasn't. As I was headed home on this walk, there was a "77" engraved into the sidewalk which was the same amount of my refund. As I walked a little further, I picked up a penny as I was comparing our refunds in my mind and this penny had a hole in the center of it. That was the first time I had ever picked up a penny that looked like that. I asked God what the penny illustrated and He told me that the $77 was two completions and would last me, but her refund amount wouldn't last. She would go through it like she had a hole in her pockets, the same as the hole in the penny.

She started spending it like water, buying for her apartment and everything else, not thinking of saving for possible hard times. One day as I was walking with God, and I met up with them on their way to Sea World with a carful. They stopped, bragged about where they were going, then her boyfriend pulled out a roll of money and flashed it at me. He smiled as though to rub in my face.

One day I asked my stepdaughter to borrow some money but she told me she didn't have any left when I knew she did. But, that was fine because I remembered what God had shown me about the penny with the hole. I knew God would take care of me, even though flesh had me worried.

Not too long after and as God had shown me, the money was gone and her lavish world had fallen apart. Early one Sunday morning I received a call to go to her house because of a shooting. Her boyfriend had shot at her babies' father when he came to pick up the kids. He could've hit the kids' father and my granddaughter, but the bullet missed them and hit the center of his car's windshield. When I got there and saw everybody was fine, I left and went to church. The police didn't want me to leave my stepdaughter by herself, but I left anyway.

Another time I was in my apartment talking to the preacher about my concern about my stepdaughter. As I was telling him I was scared, a knock came at the door telling me that my stepdaughter had just gotten beat up by that same boyfriend. A few times before she had gotten beat up by him. I went over to her apartment, saw her in pain, and took her to the hospital. All these times the police were called, but she didn't follow through by going down to the police station and filing charges. None of the incidents were on record.

When we got back from the hospital, he was rubbing it in by driving up and down the street of my ex-wife's apartment because he knew that's where my stepdaughter was staying. It had gotten so bad until the property manager barred him from coming onto the property, but she would still slip him into her apartment at night.

One day while returning home from a walk, there were three bullet casings on the ground right in front of me. They made me stop with such a fearful emotion and at first I refused to touch them, then later went back and picked them up. Those, I thought, represented my stepdaughter and her two kids' deaths. Not too long after, there was another shooting by her boyfriend. Again, I went over there, found that she was fine, but noticed that there were three bullet holes in her bedroom window (same number of bullet casings found while I was walking). That was the last straw with the property manager asked her to leave. I couldn't help or talk for her this time because of all of the incidents surrounding her boyfriend. She packed up, moved with a girlfriend, and a short time later, she and her kids moved in with my ex-wife. After a host of ups and downs with her mother, she decided she couldn't take it any more and came over to talk to me. I told her to go over to the complex office, talk to the manager again, and maybe she would give her another chance. She came back later and was very happy because the manager gave her the same apartment back. I told her to thank God because He was the only reason she got it back.

We most times allow money to rule us and alter our better judgments. God doesn't want us to be jealous of what others have. Satan has us so high and mighty when we get a little more than others. We also tend to brag and boast a little when we have a little more, looking down on ones who don't have. We want to keep it to ourselves, not remembering God blesses us to bless others. We don't realize that by blessing others, God will replace those blessing much more. When we get a little extra money, why don't we give God his share first? That's the reason we go through it so fast. The reason I left for church on the first shooting was because God had already been there and saved their lives. Everything was fine there, so I had to get to church to thank and praise Him for being there before me. If God hadn't arrived on schedule and protected my family, it could've been a very deadly outcome, especially seeing where the bullets ended up. From the point where her boyfriend started shooting and where the one landed in the windshield, my granddaughter and/or her father should have been shot. There was also one shot that was fired in the apartment's bedroom that should have struck my stepdaughter or her boyfriend, yet it went into the floor.

Satan tells us, especially the young girls, not to file charges on our close relations because we are in love with them. We don't understand that Satan is confusing us into setting up for the next happening. The time I took her to the hospital and her boyfriend was riding up and down her street, Satan had me get my gun. I felt he was rubbing his violence in my family's face, but when I got back, God stepped in and removed him from the property. Satan had her so deceived she wouldn't file charges on him and kept taking him back. When her boyfriend and my grandson were in a wreck going to the store, her boyfriend got arrested, his car was totaled, and the only thing saved was my grandson who came away unharmed. Again, God was there to protect my family because looking at that wrecked car, neither of the two should've come away alive.

When there is something or someone on our minds

wearing us down and we can't shake it loose, that is God talking to our spirits to be on the lookout of a happening that's about to come. Even when we continue to go backward, God will still give us another chance to go forward. He is so merciful and loves us so much, He continues picking us up! That's why we need to continue praising and thanking Him because where would we be?

CHAPTER NINE

New Beginnings

A: EARLY PROBLEMS

My son and I had this brand-new life starting and were very excited about not having to go through the abuse. It looked like everything was finally beginning to go our way. Two weeks later, we were pretty much settled in and suddenly, Satan brought on more obstacles. Below are some of the many things we had to overcome.

I became very depressed because the Christmas holiday had approached and I had no money to get my child any gifts. All of the other parents and kids were talking about what gifts they were going to get, which made him hopeful. Satan was reminding me of all of the times I had money and bought my stepchildren everything they desired, yet I couldn't buy the special kid God gave me a single gift. He knew where my weakness was and played on it. All I could see was my son without gifts and having no place to go because he hadn't yet established any new friends. My son didn't even have any new clothes to wear on the holiday like the other kids, but I decided as long as he had something to put on, that didn't matter.

The day before the holiday, I decided to walk with God and ask Him to make a way out of no way. I walked and cried out to God because He was my only hope and I thought that was looking pretty slim. We didn't even have enough food to eat on that holiday.

Isn't it funny how Satan reminds us of all of the things we had when we were serving him? He plays on our emotions like that just to try to deceive us back to serving him. He knows if we allow him to overcome our weaknesses, we won't trust God. But, he's so fooled himself that he doesn't know that God has everything already done.

Later that evening, my son received a phone call from his friend asking him if he wanted to go with him and his family to Corpus the next morning. I agreed to let him go because I felt at least he would have someone to play with. I was still worried I had no money to give him.

The next morning about two hours before they would leave, one of my older cousins came over, brought over gifts of new clothes and money that were sent from my son's grandmother. I knew then that God had this thing under His control and I didn't feel bad for him going. I really thanked God because he had no money and no good clothes to take with him, but God came through again. You could tell the difference in my son going from sadness to excitement. When his friend's mother drove up, I went out to see them off and began to talk to her mother who was sitting on the passenger's side. Before they drove off, the mother put some money in my hand telling me Merry Christmas. I thought it was a couple of dollars, but when I counted it after I got back into my apartment, it was almost $100. I just shouted, thanking God because not only did He take care of my son's needs, He took care of mine also giving us much more than we expected. Even when we give up, He doesn't because He already had it set up. God still wasn't finished yet because later that same night, I heard a knock on the front door and answered. When I opened the door, it was my out-of-town friend and her daughters surprising me. They started bringing in bags and bags of groceries, so many they had to set many of the bags on my floors. Also, before they left, my friend gave me a Christmas card with a $20 bill inside the envelope. God had given me almost $120 in cash and all of my kid's desires in one day. What a God we serve! He looks past our faults and supplies our need.

It had gotten to the point where we again had run out of food. I had depended on getting some groceries that my stepdaughter had bought for us because my son's name was included on her food stamp allocation. The only problem was we weren't getting our fair share because we had to depend on her with her transportation and she would just normally go shopping, yet buy us only what she thought we needed. But, then she forgot to go to an appointment and they cut her food stamps off until she reapplied. There was a real problem there because we didn't know when or if she would get them back.

One morning I realized that my son was going to come home from school and wouldn't have anything to eat for dinner. I thanked God for him being able to eat at school because at least he had eaten something. Although I was and would've been hungry, I didn't worry about myself, yet I would sacrifice for him to eat. All I could do was pray about it and depend on God. So many times He came to my rescue, so why wouldn't I believe otherwise this time?

A little later that morning, my daughter-in-law came by to visit me. She gave me a ride down to the food stamp office where I completed the paperwork. Normally, after completing the paperwork, the office will schedule the applicant a later appointment in about a month, then give out the food stamps. Not only did they give me an appointment a few hours after I turned the paperwork in, when I left their office, they had authorized me more than I expected in food stamps. They also set it up making them available for use later that night and each month thereafter, I would receive the same amount. God had set the whole thing up. He promised He'd feed us when we were hungry and give us water when we were thirst. When you're hungry, just ask God to feed you and believe that He is able to fulfill His promises to us. God had it already completed even before I asked Him.

After we got settled into our apartment, I established a walking route. God had already established that coins would be signs He would send me as I was speaking to Him about specific topics. The coins would confirm that God heard me and it was already fixed to His will and not mine. I know it seems strange and unbelievable to some, but that's our one-on-one communication tool.

One day I was walking with Him in distress about something, and normally He showed me two pennies, but this particular day I walked about three-fourths of the route and got worried if He heard me because I hadn't found a single penny. He always left me different coins with significant meanings. I looked out into this busy street and there was a penny in the middle of the pavement. After the fast cars went by, I went out there and tried to remove the asphalt stuck penny from its position. I tried every way of removing it and running back and forth to get out of the way of the speeding vehicles, but couldn't get it out of the asphalt. As I returned to finish my walk, God told me that He placed that penny there permanently because He'll always be there hearing me.

A few days later on the opposite end He told me to look in the middle of the street. I looked and there was another penny stuck in the asphalt in the middle of the pavement. I didn't try to remove it because I knew it wouldn't happen. I knew then I didn't have to worry about God touching and agreeing with me, because as long as I walked the entire route, He had the pennies at each end.

God knew that I counted on getting those signs and knew the coins confirmed Him touching and agreeing with me. When I walked, there was nobody but He and I, so I needed Him to touch and agree with me. He placed one at each end of this mile-long route and buried them in asphalt so they'd be there even if I didn't find any other coins. What are the chances of that happening? Flesh wouldn't have been able to see this, but when you're trying to walk with God in the Spirit, then those things will be obvious to you. A personal relationship with God has nothing to do with anyone else but God and you. It's an intimacy that only God can provide for us. It doesn't matter if flesh thinks or believes that you are crazy when you're talking to God. He wanted me to know even with the fast traffic of life (our problems) and our earlier seeds planted, God is still asphalted in our souls and cannot be moved.

My first CPS utility bill came and I didn't have the money to pay for it, so I didn't pay it. The second bill came and it informed me that if I didn't pay it by a certain date, they were going to turn off my electricity. I only had $40 to my name, so I asked my older stepdaughter to borrow the money and she claimed she didn't have any. I didn't make any more calls because I didn't have a personal phone and didn't have the money to use the pay phones. Even if I did have the payphone money, I was limited to whom I could call. So I walked and told God about it. He told me to go over to my stepdaughter, use her phone, and tell the telephone employee I would pay the amount due the following Tuesday.

Now, this was Friday and the only thing that would change between the two days was God had to do it, especially on a weekend. The entire weekend through Monday afternoon had passed and I hadn't gotten the money for the bill. I began to stress out because I was certain they would cut it off if I didn't take them the money the next day. So I walked again telling God my dire situation that was running out of time. About 8 p.m., I braced myself for the worst and made plans of how we were going to operate without electricity. Someone also had told me that the complex management would evict you if they found out your electricity was turned off. I had all of that on my mind. The utility company said when I called that Friday that my $40 wasn't enough, and they needed $240 by the following Tuesday to keep it on. Around 8:30 p.m., I decided to go outside and call my son to come inside to get ready for school the next day. I called him in and just as I was about to shut the door, I heard this voice call my name. I looked back out and saw this white couple backing out of a parking space, then pull back in. They got out of the car and instantly I recognized them. It was my old boss with his wife whom I hadn't seen in about seven years. We embraced each other and he told me he had looked all over for me because he needed me to witness an incident for my old company. As I was telling him I would do it, I saw his wife scratching out some writing in her checkbook. He looked at her and asked her if she wrote it, with her telling him no, that I probably needed cash. He told me that they had to make a run but they would be back shortly.

They left and I went into my apartment kind of puzzled. About thirty minutes later, he knocked on my door and when I opened it, he reached me $200 in cash. He told me that was for helping my old company out. We again embraced each other, he left, and I just started praising God because I had the exact amount of money I promised the utility company I would pay the following day.

There is no doubt that God had everything planned out. How was I to know that my ex-boss was going to bring me the balance of the money? God also knew the amount of money I had when I made the call and then put obstacles in my ex-boss's way so he couldn't find me until that appointed late Monday night. He waits right to the end because He wants us to realize that it had to be Him to bring us through each situation when we give up. By doing it that way, He knows He will get bigger and more heartfelt praise from us. There was no way my ex-boss could have known that I needed $200 for my bill. Also, if I would've gone out of my door three minutes later, I would've missed them but it was God's timing and not mine. Seven means completion and by me not seeing my ex-boss for seven years, he was the one for God to use to fulfill His promise of Tuesday. That mission was completed. Isn't it wonderful to see that God is so detailed and has an anointed time for each step of His plan?

He could've given me all of it that Friday, but He wanted

to see my reactions leading up to when He finally gave it to me. If we can ever completely trust God and have faith that it's already done before we ask, we'll eliminate all our worries. Here again like the angel in the story of Abraham, my ex-boss was my ram in the bush. Doesn't Satan ever get tired of placing obstacles in our path knowing from much experience that God has already removed them? The answer is no, because he doesn't know God's plan, but should realize God's power will surpass any obstacle.

When we first got our apartment, a family friend had signed for us a telephone. When she ordered the service, I told her to order only a dial tone because I knew I could come up with that much money. I didn't know at the time that some costly features automatically came with the activation unless you tell them to eliminate them. I don't think our friend knew about this either. My younger stepdaughter would always come over and talk to her friends on the three-way feature with me being ignorant of the fact that it was costing me. She would also use the trace feature to see who had just called and hung up, again not knowing it was costing me. When I received the bill, I was outraged because there was no way I could come up with the amount charged because of those features. I called the company and argued the charges and they decreased my bill a little, but not to the point I was able to pay it. A little later, they disconnected the phone because of failure to pay the bill. I needed a phone because my son was in school and if he had an accident, they couldn't contact me. Also, my handicapped brother was in a center and they needed to be able to call me if something would happen.

I tried to call anyone I thought would get me a phone line, but no one I asked would do it. I walked and talked to God because everything I tried failed. During each walk, there was this broken phone at the curb of an intersection and it was there each time I passed. I knew it represented my phone and I knew that when I didn't see it anymore, I would get my phone. It had gotten to a point that I would get so frustrated by seeing it there. I didn't ever touch it because I knew that was the sign from God.

A few months later, my next-door neighbor came over and told me she had applied for a phone, that she had prayed that the ones I tried to get wouldn't succeed. She said she wanted to get it because she could get a discount for me. A few days later, I had a phone and I just praised God because He heard my neighbor's prayer. I went on a walk that same day, passed the intersection where the broken phone was, and it was gone. God already knew my need and had already set it up.

God knew I got my initial phone through my own will. That's the reason that one got shut off. I allowed my friend to set up the service instead of allowing God to set it up because God would've known about those hidden costly features. Any time we try to do something on our own after asking God to do it, our actions always fail in the long run. Satan tricks us into believing we can do it without God's help because he knows we tend not to have patience to wait on God. Satan knows that patience is one of our favorite weaknesses. If I would've picked up the broken phone and thrown it away, I would've broken the belief that it was a sign from God. I knew that God had left it there to show me to have faith. Also, my neighbor probably said her prayer the same time I saw the broken phone by that curb. Not only did I get the line I asked for, but it cost me about a third of what it would've cost if I or the people I called got the line ourselves. God's way cost me much less than I could afford to pay. His ways are not our ways!

During this process, Satan would always show me the unsaved with cell and house phones trying to get me envious of them and turn on God. Satan will use our impatience against us including getting us involved illegally.

When we moved in, I brought my computer that was broken with the hard drive really messed up. It also would turn off by itself. I set up half of my bedroom closet as a mini-office and I needed my computer to work properly. I did everything I knew to fix it but it wouldn't even accept the internet when I would try to install it. It really got me so frustrated one day, I thought about taking it to the dumpster and throwing it away. Instead of doing that, I decided to pray and give God a chance. I tried to call repair people I found in the newspaper, but either they were too expensive or tried to walk me through the repair that didn't work. After I failed at trying to correct it, I stood back, used patience, and allowed God to answer my prayer, no matter how small. It had gotten so frustrating, I deleted too much causing my whole computer to crash and needed to reprogram the whole thing. I didn't have the setup CD and all of the ones I borrowed didn't work. My other option was to buy the CD from a store, but I didn't have the money.

Immediately, God placed this girl who used to work for me on my mind giving me that direction to call. The timing was excellent because the same time I made the call, there was one of her employees standing beside her who had a CD. A few days later, I picked it up at her store, came home, installed it, and it worked perfectly fixing my computer. I was also able to install the internet without any problems.

God will bless us with anything that is of His will and all we have to do is ask. God knew my desire led me to frustration toward my computer and also knew that I'd done all that I could do to fix it, but needed a greater answer. Most times we ask God for help with our physical body, materialistic things, interventions, etc., but hardly ever do we ask him to repair things that are broken. We'll just give up and try to replace it with a new one. God controls everything. He can do it. He will give us the desires of our hearts no matter how small our requests. God knew the exact time that guy would be at the store and the exact person for me to call. What are the chances that he would be there at that time and have the exact CD that I needed if it wasn't God? If we trust God with our large prayers, do we think He's too busy to answer the small ones? The computer was a special blessing anyways. After I turned it over to God, unexpectedly my daughter had a brand new computer just sitting at home, which she gave me. Not only did she give me the computer, she gave me a new printer also. God let me go through all of those disappointments because I was trying to do it. As soon as I couldn't do it, it's like He said if I would've just waited or trusted Him from the beginning, He already had a complete one for me at my daughter's house. Then I wouldn't have gone through all of those disappointments.

When we moved in, I also brought my fifty-gallon fish aquarium. I had done away with the few fish I had and poured all of its gravel in a flowerbed. After getting my apartment set up, I had an empty aquarium sitting there. It looked bad but I had no money to buy the fish or the gravel. God knew it was really bothering me but I couldn't do anything about it. One night my daughter-in-law came by for a visit and my son convinced her to take him to the store. About an hour after they left, I thought about the gravel but didn't want to ask her to buy it because I had no money to repay her. I called her on her cell phone and when she answered she told me they had just checked out and were on their way back to my house. I started to ask her but declined because they had already finished with their purchases. I just felt that God didn't want me to have it at that time, so I just accepted it.

When they got home, my daughter-in-law gave me a bag, and there were three or four bags of gravel in the bag. I didn't even suggest in any way for her to buy the gravel and never would I have guessed that the same time we were on the phone, she was buying my desire. It didn't look like that was enough gravel to cover even the bottom of the aquarium. After spreading the bags, the amount was perfect. Also, I then needed some fish, so my stepdaughter hesitantly gave me two and the preacher gave me two. I was satisfied with the number of fish, but about a week later, my stepdaughter had broken her aquarium and she had to give me a lot more so they wouldn't die. After that, my aquarium was perfect.

God had the gravel already set up before I even asked about it. My daughter-in-law hadn't even planned to stop by for the visit, let alone did she plan to buy aquarium gravel. The thing I didn't know was that asking God was enough. We need to stop underestimating God even with our smallest prayers. This is a sure example of asking, forgetting, and having faith it will be done. I was embarrassed to ask her to buy the gravel, but God wasn't. It was like after mentioning the gravel at my house, God made my daughter-in-law go to the store and specifically buy the gravel because they were going there to buy my son a toy. She certainly didn't know how much would cover the bottom of the aquarium, but she purchased the exact amount needed. My stepdaughter really didn't want to give me any of the many fish she had, but after hesitantly giving me two, her aquarium broke. Then she was forced to give me the rest. God blessed us to bless others and not be selfish. God will replace all that we give to others in need more and abundantly. There is none who can beat God's giving. We need to be careful when someone asks us for something because God may have sent them to us just to see if we will share. Most times when we have more than what we need, we sometimes get greedy and forget everything is God's anyway. We forget we can lose it in a split second and be in the same position as the one who is asking. If we become too selfish with the blessings God gives us and we don't praise Him for giving them, He'll take them away from us. Satan will deceive you into thinking all you have belongs to you and not God.

When I got a promotion years ago, I bought this gold nugget ring with a horseshoe on the top. They had convinced me that horseshoes represented luck and back in those days, I was in the world not knowing the difference. I really believed that it was my lucky charm wearing the ring. That ring was my pride and joy. When bad times hit, I had no choice but to pawn the ring for money. As the following years past, I would put it in and take it out of the pawnshop each time I was strapped for money. Each time I let it go past the pick-up date and they were about to sell it, somehow I would find the money to get it out. The last time I pawned it, I was unable to get it out and the pawnshop sold it. The sale of my good luck ring devastated me so much. I prayed to God. I would see a likeness in the paper and ask my kids to get it for me on holidays, but they never did. I settled to the fact that I wasn't going to get one.

One Christmas morning, my neighbor brought me a gift from her and her kids and when I opened it, they had given me a gold ring with a cross on top. It was beautiful and I liked it so much, I wouldn't remove it even to be sized. I was thankful, but it still didn't feel like a replacement to the one I lost.

A few months later while that same neighbor and I were walking in a store, something told me to go over to the jewelry counter. Immediately after we got there and looked inside the glass case, there was a gold nugget ring with a gold cross. I knew right away that was the ring and we immediately went back to her house and picked up the receipt of the old one, then traded the old one in for the new nugget ring. When I put it on my finger, I knew it was the one and God had blessed me again with my desire.

When I truly started trying to walk with God I lost my ring. God knew I was placing that ring before Him and He wasn't going to have it. He knew Satan had confused my mind into thinking "luck" is real. There is no such thing as "luck" when you're walking with God. Everything that happens to the ones trying to walk with God is because of His will and not man's luck. He means to give you every large and small blessing you get and it's not because you're just lucky. If you truly allow Him to guide your footsteps, it is not luck in your actions. On this ring, God gave me back everything I had except He exchanged the horseshoe of luck for the cross of life. He exchanged luck for His blood. The reason my kids wouldn't buy me the rings was that God already had the one He wanted me to have. Our lack of patience stimulates our worst fears when we walk with God and do not trust Him.

There were many days I would need money, even after giving my last to someone who seemed to need it more than me, and I wouldn't know where the next dollar would come from. I was blessed with the use of my cousin's Cadillac for a few months before the transmission went out. I didn't have the money to get it repaired, so they pulled it off and sold it. This car took my followers and me to/from church, took my neighbor and close relatives to their destinations, took my son to and from school, but used lots of oils and gasoline in its operation. During that time, gasoline prices were at a record high. It really looked bad on the outside and the inside, but it got us to our destinations. It stopped running the same time I got the sign to stop going to this church that had lots of problems, which was a conformation in itself. Each time I wouldn't have gas money to go to Bible study or church, someone would come by and give me a few dollars or have me to take them somewhere putting enough gas in the car for their trips and my travels to/from church. This never failed to occur all of the days I drove the car.

One morning this lady needed to make this food stamp appointment because if she didn't, she would have to reapply and would have to wait months for the next appointment. She was already strapped for money and food for her kids and missing it would hurt her family. She didn't have any money and all I had was eight dollars, but her family needed it more than I needed it. So I took my last, borrowed a friend's truck, put gas in it, took her to the appointment, brought her back, and used the last few dollars to get her kid something to eat. I knew somehow God would supply me if I needed that money later because He hadn't failed me before.

Later that evening as we were sitting on my porch talking about Jesus, and this female stranger called me over to an empty field. I had only been greeting her each day as she went to and from her job. When I got there, she asked me to open my hand as she put some paper into it, then told me to close my hand as though it was a secret. So I closed my hand, put the paper into my pocket, and went back to the porch resuming my conversation. Later on that evening while in my bedroom, I pulled out the paper the stranger had given me, and to my surprise she had given me eight dollars. Not only money, but there have been material needs that has been given to me unexpectedly.

God not only waits a lot of the time until the last minutes to bless us, but He surprises us with blessings as added favor. There is no doubt God knows and supplies our needs/desires down to the details. The Cadillac had run its course and had done the job God wanted it to do.

When it stopped, it wasn't surprising, nor did I get upset because I was out of transportation. Sure I would've loved the transportation, but that was God's will and timing. I felt when God was ready for me to have other transportation, He would give it to me. Many times afterwards, I would ask God for forgiveness for being envious and jealous of others having transportation and not me. It would really trouble me when I would see people sinning, yet driving nice vehicles and here I was trying to walk with God having none. Many times God doesn't bless us when we think He should because He has something better for us in the future. Then when He does bless us, we look back and see it was better to wait. Many times, God will allow us to lean on our own understanding and allow us to do it before He was ready just to show us it doesn't last. When we allow God to do it for us in His own time, it always lasts. If God knows the number of hairs on our heads, He knows everything about us. God knew I had given my last to the lady in need and He returned those same eight dollars through a stranger. God uses others to bless us. If I wouldn't have blessed the lady with my last, I probably would've used my eight dollars and struggled afterwards. If you always give freely from your heart, I promise God will make it up to you in more ways you can't imagine. You need to keep giving if you have selfish motives that don't directly come from a pure and cheerful heart. People in need don't need selfishness or sympathy, they just need sincere help. Don't confuse "giving" with a "loan" because the definition is very different.

The anointing with oil is very sacred symbolic act to me because the Bible tells us to do so. Olives were special in the old days because they were used as food and pressed down for the oil to prepare the food. So when you anoint someone, you are about to "feed" them with the Word (God). I try very hard to keep some blessed oil on hand at all times. I was given this little bottle from a minister one day filled with blessed oil and when I felt the anointing from God, I knew it was real. When I would run low, I would fill the bottle back up with the oil at church because I felt it was blessed. This bottle is small, thin, and can fit in the palm of your hand, which makes it easy to carry. Since I've lived in the apartment, I've bought a larger bottle to refill the smaller one after praying over the larger one for seven days (completion). The smaller bottle was full when I left the church and I have used a little over half to anoint some lost people before praying for them. It's not the oil itself, but it's your belief that the oil is a symbol of God.

Something happened to me one day walking my route with God that was overwhelming and so awesome. I always carry my little bottle of oil with me as I walk my route with God because it gives me a sense of protection and I never know whom God will put in my path to pray for and anoint.

One day I looked at the oil in the little bottle to see if I needed to refill it and found the shock of my life. The oil in the bottle had turned clear as water, yet it had started out being yellow. I couldn't believe my eyes and asked others if that had ever happened to them. Also, I've used out of that bottle many times and it seemed to refill back to the point when I noticed the color change. I wouldn't have believed it unless I saw it for myself and it is still clear and refilling itself. Many other times I would walk and by the time I got back, my hand holding the bottle would be soaked with oil, even with the top of the bottle screwed tight. One day a friend witnessed it, too. It was like there were holes in the bottle that allowed the oil to seep out. Maybe there is another explanation, but I don't think so because the larger bottle of oil I purchased has not changed colors and is still yellow.

Again, there is nothing impossible when it comes to God. He'll show you things that are mind-boggling. I believe that with my strong belief and faith in the oil and God, He had to show me His extraordinary power. The bottle has never again run out, yet refills because God is showing me that when He touches something, there's a change and His proof is without question. Why do we always expect less? He's shown me spoons, then forks and knives during my walks with Him. He's shown me fruit seeds, describing that the seed my mother and grandmother planted in me. He's shown me sticks shaped as "Y's" to let me know that my stepmother was thinking of me. He showed me a breastplate one day letting me know people can hurt my body but they cannot penetrate my soul because He's protecting me.

We all know that the heart is the primary organ of our

body that pumps all of our blood throughout and if someone kills it, they kill the entire body. Also, that's where all of our emotions come from and love is the key. That's why we say that our heart has to be right for our actions to be sincere. He has shown me dead birds in my path letting me know not to worry about others, let the dead bury the dead. He sends people with messages from Him.

One day I was troubled about something taking too long and immediately a car passed with this lady sticking her head out of her window telling me that God said "it won't be long." It was a split second after saying the words to God that she said that and she didn't really know me. These are just a few of the signs and wonders God has shown me during my intimate walks with Him. God just wants you to spend some intimate time with Him so He can reveal some things and show you just how much He loves you. Remember, when you put oil onto someone, you need to make sure that the setting is about none other than God and have the faith that you're feeding the Word. Of course, you need to make sure that you are of God before doing so because if not, you're wasting time. Pretending this is playing with God!

When we try our best to walk with God, don't think that when your life gets better, all of your challenges are gone. On the contrary, they get harder because you are tested all the time to see if you truly believe in God. Sometimes Satan has us in such confusion, we forget about thanking

God for our big blessings, let alone the small ones. People who don't believe that God is real are only alive in the flesh and not in the spirit. God reveals Himself in many ways and unless you are spirit-filled, you will believe in coincidence and luck. All of the above are personal and real proof that God is real. When you find no other explanation, why not give God His due credit? The stories in the Bible lives on today in our current lives proving to us that His Words are life. God proves Himself to us just so we can go out and tell others how great He really is. Doubting His Word is denying His existence.

B: LOST LAMB ATTRACTIONS

Jesus said, "If I am lifted up, I'll draw men neigh to me" and not if flesh is lifted up, people will come running. Many of us think by us having a religious title, we can get lost souls to follow us. That is so far from the truth because even respect has to be gained and not given. You can't use I, my, me, etc., when you're trying to bring God's people closer to Him. It's not about you because you are only supposed to be God's vessel and not God Himself. You cannot boast and think that the lost lambs are going to bow down to you. They may at first, but God will reveal your realness to them. We sometimes think that the lost are stupid and don't recognize that most of them had a seed planted in them at their early age. That's why it surprises you when you start talking to them about God and they begin to quote scripture, tell Bible stories, and hold a spiritual conversation with you. The only thing separating them, like all of us, is there hasn't been anyone taking the time to water their seeds. When they were born, God had a purpose for them just as He did for us. The only reason we have gotten through some of our lost situations is so we can help those lost through theirs. God knew when He brought us out of our mess He had someone coming around in the future. How can we really help someone out of their mess if we haven't gone through the same mess they're in? If you're truly trying to walk with God and He lives in you, the attraction will be there. They may not be able to explain it, but they know there's something different about you that makes you stand out in love and peace.

When people come and want to hang around you all of the time, they are not drawn to the fleshly you, it's the Jesus in you. With His lost lambs, God will give you the words to say to them because He already knows their hurts and everything they need. He can't do that with you being "holier than thou." There are many people saying that God told them to do this or that and when they do this or that, they have no followers. These people don't understand and never question whether it was really God they heard. They definitely are not going to question themselves because of their own pride. If something you thought God told you to do doesn't produce fruit, then it was not from God.

God's plans are perfect and if He truly tells you to do something, the moment He tells you, the fruits are already waiting. Some people just don't get it, yet they continue to lean on their own understanding. The lost lambs they convince to join them become more lost. *Woe unto the shepherds who scatters my sheep.* You also have to be so careful when you turn your back on someone because you don't know their hurt, nor do you know if God put them in your path for help. Turning your back on them is like turning your back on Jesus. Satan will set you up thinking that it was from God because he knows your weakness is all about self. God will use you to prove Himself to the lost lambs if everything in you is about Him. It is not productive for the lost lambs to hear about your problems because they have enough of their own. When you encounter a lost lamb, don't initially give them advice, take as much time as they need and listen. The deep hurt inside needs to come out without interruption so you can feel what they feel. The lost lambs will truthfully open up to you about their hurt because emotions come from the heart. Interjecting too quickly or pushing them with words in any way will make them lose interest and damage them more. Many times they just needs someone to talk to. That's why you want God to lead you and all you have to do is ask God what to say before saying anything.

Never judge a hurt by its outside appearance because the price of recovered pain is just too high. Judging them initially will alter your best efforts of compassion to their needs and ultimately say or demand the wrong thing to or from them. If it's an obvious sinful act, remember God loves them just as much as he loves you. He just doesn't love their sin. Their sin is probably the reason God sent them your way. In fact, if you're walking with God and trying to do His will, He has so many lost souls being sent your way, you'll get physically tired. That's when you have to suck it up, ask God for strength, and continue ministering to them. You can tell the instant God gives you the strength because all of a sudden, the discussion will get so exciting you'll want to shout. You will also be able to tell that God used you as His vessel by the humble gratitude shown by the lost soul. You'll be able to tell without a doubt that God, through you, spoke to them, giving them the hope they were looking for.

C: CHANGING LOST LIVES

After I was in the apartment complex area for about a month, I realized then God placed me there for His purpose. There were many lost souls residing on the complex property and it reminded me of a Sodom and Gomorrah. There were men trying to be women, women trying to be men, all sexes selling their bodies, all kinds of drugs, gang problems, shootings, stabbings, killings, child abuse, etc., that openly occurred without shame. This was a place you would certainly stay away from if it were your choice. I knew there was nobody in the flesh who could change this place, but had to depend on God's Word and His guidance to cause the necessary changes. Satan and his demons had the place locked up with sin from one end to the other. I started sitting on my front porch so I could see what was going on around me. Then I began to just speak and smile to everyone passing by. All of a sudden in a very short time, people started stopping and sitting on my porch. I would listen to them and most of them just wanted a listening ear, and eventually they'd talk about Jesus. A short time later, I had a porch full of people, which kept me out on the porch from morning until dawn. As soon as a few would leave, others would come. There would be people who stopped in the middle of the street just to talk because, without understanding, they knew there was something special happening on my porch. There were prayers prayed, testimonies shared, life-long stories told, and everything required bringing down the Holy Spirit on that porch. Satan and his demons would come close and sometimes touch the porch, but they had to leave immediately because there was too much God there.

This is still going on even up to the date of this writing. When people would be uplifted in prayer at the bus stop, in the streets, or on the porch, it seemed like that prayer would echo all over the property. People who were passing by would literally stop what they were doing to listen to the prayer. The people passing by the porch would stop, raise their hands to the sky, and just thank God. When God's

Word goes out, it doesn't come back void. All of a sudden, God's reputation through me spread throughout the complex. I had people speaking to me and titling me Deacon, Deac, Rev, or Preacher. There were so many women on my porch I was labeled as a pimp twice. One of them had the nerve to warn me concerning territory and that I needed to be careful. What he didn't know was that I had Jesus on my side protecting me. Also, he wasn't threatening me, but he was doing it to Jesus. Who was he to tell Jesus where He can be and where He can't be? Greater is He that's in me, than he that's in the world, which gives me a hedge of protection around me.

Even the property maintenance personnel came to the porch for personal and property related prayers.

There is no doubt that the ones we prayed for did indeed experience the presence of God during those prayers. All of them said they felt something.

Before I met my neighbor, I was hesitant because of some of her behaviors. I heard her cursing, screaming, etc., with visitors. Even with that I felt a good heart inside her because of the care she showed with her kids. If she had something to do, whether in the heat, cold, or rain, she would get her kids together and catch the bus, not bothering anyone. Finally I introduced myself to her and invited her to go with me to church. She accepted and went with me every Sunday afterwards until we left the church. Then she started joining the group on my porch every day where she would get words from God. She began to confide in me all of the things God was revealing to her, mostly concerning her friends and acquaintances. She was the most "giving from the heart" person that I had ever met. She did things for people expecting nothing in return. Unfortunately, most of those people used her kindness for their benefit, taking complete advantage of her goodness. She would give them money, household supplies, gasoline, groceries and everything that they needed.

The first thing I told her was to close the door on the usage and trust nobody but Jesus. Those people didn't like what she started doing, so they began to stray away. Almost every day God would use me to tell her how to get out of her creation and not miss the friendship she thought she had. Although she was missing the friendships, she was gaining a greater friend in Jesus.

She had also applied for SSI because of an illness she suffered, but it seemed like she was always going through the government red tape. She only had to depend on the little money she would get for her kids stretching it to make ends meet. She developed a personal relationship with God, thanking and praising Him as a routine throughout the day. She's currently allowing God to guide her in every area of her life and most of all she's not ashamed to let people know who is guiding her. She lifts Jesus up daily.

The words of God became her true friend and He proved Himself by confirmations and deliveries. Somewhere in her earlier life, someone planted a seed and all God did through me was water that seed with His Words. When she started really walking with God, not only did He reveal things in her own life, but with others too. Her giving was genuine from her heart and not selfish to make herself look good. God saw her heart and started blessing her accordingly because she gave Him all of the praise. Her transformation was awesome. God took the void for her user friends from her and filled it with His presence. God blessed her with her own vehicle so she and her kids wouldn't have to walk or ride the bus again in the bad weather. God blessed her where she didn't need to babysit her so-called friends' kids for money. God removed the government red tape and ordered her an SSI check to come the rest of her natural life. Every time she needs anything, God always came through giving her the desires of her heart. She's also planting good seeds into her kids so they will grow up and produce good fruit. God has even blessed her with a stronger relationship with her mother. You hardly ever see my neighbor worry anymore, because God has given her peace. She is certainly the ultimate example of God blessing us to bless others. When things come up against her, she doesn't count on man, yet her favorite words are, "Jesus got this so I'm not worried." By her total belief, faith, and trust in God, He has opened up the windows of Heaven and is pouring down blessings she can't hold. When she talks about Jesus, the smile on her face definitely comes from her sincere heart. God has used her to draw others closer to Him because He's contagious.

Almost every time I went on my walks, I would see this retired military guy who was always by himself. It didn't seem like he had any close friends other than the few I saw him occasionally talking to in the street. He projected this selfish, headstrong, superior, ladies' man image, and arrogant attitude. He loved to drink his beer, yet sometimes you would see him drinking a little bottle of gin. It appeared that in the mornings he would handle all of his business, then in the evenings he would start drinking until he got drunk. I began to speak to him as I passed by him or when he would walk toward his apartment. The more I spoke, the friendlier he became toward me. He slowly inched his way onto the porch, then later joined the regulars who sat there on a daily basis. He became a part of that group.

Most of the times he sat, he would bring and drink his beer, but we would have good conversation. The more he came, the more he was digesting the Word of God. The preacher of the church I attended would come over, but would leave most of the times this lost soul would come over drinking. The preacher said he didn't want to be a part of his drinking or a bar atmosphere, yet he accepted his money when this guy once attended his church. This guy and I became very close friends and he felt the "con game" of this preacher refusing to go back to his church. I would sit out on my porch late into the night listening to his heart covered by his drunken fleshly body. He even started going to church with me every Sunday and bringing his wife. He enjoyed God's Word and put aside his selfishness and began to participate in the church functions. He told me he wanted to become a deacon in a church because he enjoyed leadership positions. Why not be a leader for God?

I began to see the changes in him because he started helping those who had done him wrong in the past. He talked about Jesus, cut down on his drinking, gave without expecting anything in return, limited his bragging on all he had achieved and gave people the benefit of doubt without judgment. He finally moved from the complex, but there is no doubt in my mind, the seeds that were planted will remain and one day he'll stop the drunkenness allowing God to use him completely.

The Bible teaches us not to judge our fellow brothers and sisters. We sometimes forget that all of us were born in sin and we are still sinning in one way or another. That's why God gave us the out of repentance because He knew none of us were perfect. Most of us won't admit our sins or it's not as open as others, yet you can't hide it from God. The ones who are open are only telling us they have some problems and need our help. Drunkenness is the sin, not drinking and the reason most of us don't drink is because we know we're not strong enough to stop before it gets to drunkenness. Satan sets you up in believing you can control the drinking, yet the atmosphere almost always takes you to the next level. This level normally dominates your speech, behavior, and attitude, leading you into more sinful areas.

Jesus never turned His back on the sinners or anyone else, so why should we? Jesus is the example we are striving to be like. When He was sitting with the sinners and they asked His disciples why, Jesus told them He came for the sinners because they were the ones needing Him, not the whole. The whole don't need a physician. The preacher said he stopped because he couldn't stand the smell of the beer. By his stopping, he never found out that this man's desire was to become a leader for God. Sometimes we "holier than thou" forget where we came from. We forget we used to smell the same way. Some of us so-called Christians probably still do drink and get drunk, but we clean ourselves up before we approach others.

I couldn't stop my friend from drinking and getting drunk, but Jesus could. My only job was to try to get him to form a personal relationship with Jesus, then allow Jesus to fix the rest. If I could do that, then it is worth going through it. One thing I noticed was that drunkenness made his heart talk about hurts or desires that had been shut down for a long time. During all of those late nights, I wasn't listening to my physical friend, but I was listening to his spiritual heart which told different stories. We write people off too fast because we are too holy or think we're better than those who really hurt inside. We don't allow ourselves to understand that maybe they want to change but don't know how. We forget that God pulled us out of our drunkenness just so He could send people like my friend to us to let them know the only answer they have is God. Jesus said if you are ashamed of me, then He's be ashamed of you to His Father. We need to reopen up our own closet doors and review all of those sins, remembering them so we won't turn our backs on others who are lost. Why is it easier to accept their money and not their souls? Putting greed before the soul is disbelief in God's Word.

Jesus told the disciples to go out unto the world and not to worry because all that they needed would already be there. His main goal was getting the lost saved and all the others would be added unto them. It's all about money and not soul saving in lots of the churches. Many churches won't allow memberships if those seeking can't pay their required tithes.

All of a sudden, God began to bless my friend with things that he had desired but thought he'd never get. With his blessings, he began without hesitation to bless others. He began to watch and cut back on his curse words. He would regulate how he treated the women in his presence, he was aware of how much he was drinking, he became a better husband, understanding that God was with him. He learned that you don't have to settle for half best with God, yet expect the best.

We must remember that an overnight healing is only in God's hands. When the lost slip back or don't quit right away, don't get discouraged because God's ways are not our ways. Just be thankful and honored that God used you as a vessel directly from Him to help Him in His plan.

That is an honor in itself. Always remember God can change the most wicked of the wicked because He changed us. Satan knew when my friend was inching over to the porch he was losing control over him. He knew he had him as long as he stayed to himself getting drunk.

Early one morning around 1 a.m., a friend and I were sitting on my porch talking about the neighborhood problems and associating them with the corrections from God. Suddenly, a young man walked around the corner about five feet from where we were sitting and greeted us. He was in a fast food uniform, carrying a forty-ounce bottle of beer, very drunk and staggering in his walk, seemingly happy. He headed to the back set of our apartments. He stopped in front of us and asked us for a hug which both of us gave him one. Then we started harassing him about his stumbling walk and he just laughed, telling us he could walk straight and all kinds of ways. Just before he walked off, he again asked us for another hug and both of us gave him one. When he was walking off, he stopped, turned back looking at us, and told us that we were good people to give a stranger a hug.

We told him God blessed him as he walked out of our sight. A little later, I walked my friend home and when I was about to return home, we heard a gunshot. On my walk home, I saw emergency vehicles all in the area this kid had walked to. I walked over to the scene, passed these two guys acting hyper and one at the corner of an apartment looking like he was hiding something or adjusting something under his shirt. It gave me an uncomfortable feeling, but I just left and walked home.

The next day on my walk, I discovered that the kid that walked past us the previous night wanting the hugs was the one who got killed about thirty minutes after he left us. There was a lot of speculation on the reason why he got killed and why he would travel my way when there was a straight shot from the bus stop to where he ended up.

There was a definite reason why God led this kid our way because he had to circle through other apartments to end up in front of mine. Even in his drunken state, I believe God was telling him that He still loved him even on his last walk to death. Perhaps the God in us gave him peace with our hugs and let him know it was going to be fine. I don't know if he knew that would be his last walk, but to ask two strangers for two hugs shows that there was something heavy on his mind even in his drunk condition. I also found out he was a grandson of a preacher who probably sowed a seed into this kid. If he did unconsciously know and needed some assurance that it would be fine, God probably told him that there were two of His vessels sitting outside that would show him that He still loved him. This kid wasn't really hugging us, he was hugging the Jesus in us. The hugs were probably confirmation that the kid was forgiven and it was fine to come on home. What would've happened if we had elected not to give the young man the hugs? We didn't know he was walking to his death in a matter of minutes. God elected to send him our way because He knew we weren't going to turn him away. This incident strongly showed me we have to be very careful of turning our backs on people because we never know if they're on their last day on earth. We have to switch our judging to loving! God also kept us outside until the kid arrived.

Late one evening while I was talking to a friend about God, a thin, short white girl came up to us. She looked at me and interrupted our conversation by saying she was looking for someone. Being irritated, I turned to her and told her that it wasn't me that she was looking for, then returned to my conversation. We continued our conversation and by us ignoring the girl, she turned slowly, walking away. Afterwards, I would see her in the neighborhood walking around the property, catching rides, and most times looking like she was lost. I still didn't say anything, nor did I even speak, but knew she was the one I had turned away. I don't know if I felt that she was too dirty to talk to, if she was just another drug addict looking for a fix, or what made me not want to be around her, but I was wrong. I was wrong because I was judging her.

About a week later, I had gotten up by the corner store and saw this same girl sitting on the curb with a cigarette that she had picked up off of the street. As I was passing her, she asked me for a light and hesitantly, I gave her one. I continued my walk while she sat back down on the curb and as I approached the edge of the main street, God told me to go ask her if I could pray for her. There were other cars in the store's parking lot, so I hesitated but walked up to her and asked. She hesitated at first but accepted my request and I prayed for her. Afterwards, I went back to the same edge of the street and God told me to look back at her. I turned and looked at her in her dirty clothes, with her head down, probably homeless, probably hungry, probably no money and smoking that old cigarette she had found on the street. I turned my head back in front of me wondering what God was telling me to look at. Then He said, *Don't you remember that was you just a year ago?* I felt so bad because I turned my back on someone who just the previous year was a reflection of me. The previous year I was dirty, had my head down, didn't have a home, was always hungry, had no money, and picked up cigarettes off the street to smoke. I also had someone to pray for me. We were the same, just in different bodies.

Jesus wasn't too busy for the two blind men, the old woman with the twelve-year blood disease, the leper, the multitudes, or any of the ones He took time to heal or preach to. We have to slow down and not get too busy to listen to others' hurts. The first time God sent her in my path, I was too busy talking about something that could've waited. When she said she was looking for someone and I said "Not me," she was really looking for the Jesus in me, yet I didn't really hear her. We want God to stop what He's doing to hear our every prayer, probably interrupting Him more than we should. I know He stops and listens, as proved with all of the blessings given because of our prayers. There is no topic more interesting than showing a lost soul how to become un-lost.

I got another chance to obey God with her when He sent her back my way. When she was in my presence the first time, I was doing a little better so I forgot or didn't think of my recent past. When I saw her on the curb the second time, I thought, here we go again, still having this negative demeanor. When God tells us to do something, we better be obedient and that's why I went over and prayed for her. It shouldn't matter where or when we have to uplift lost souls, especially knowing they're unable to do it themselves. That's why God puts them in our paths. God has His own way of reminding us where we've been and who pulled us out. Don't forget your past because God will show you a mirror in someone else's life.

Sometimes when God blesses us by making our lives a little better, we tend to look down or shy away from the ones who haven't made a turn yet. Jesus was compassionate all the way to the cross. What's our excuse except selfishness, uncaring, forgetfulness, and pride? This experience certainly showed me how the hurt, lost souls go to different churches for help and they are turned away or ignored. No matter how big the church is, there should be someone ordained who can help them with their cries. If we as disciples in the streets and the churches turn our backs and don't listen, to whom do the lost look toward? It's no wonder they turn back to Satan or never get away from him because he'll always be there to welcome them or hold onto them in his kingdom. Satan feels the more for him, the less for God and we're just sitting back allowing it to happen. What we don't understand is that we're not building up the kingdom of God when we turn our backs. If we listen and help that one, he/she will tell someone else who will tell another, and soon that one has multiplied to many and all for God and not Satan.

One day I was on a walk talking to God and as I passed this bus stop, there was this thin-framed black female sitting there. It was the Mother's Day holiday and all she did was smile as I walked by the bench. As soon as I passed by, she called me and asked me if I had forgotten something. She was a stranger whom I had never seen before, yet I stopped anyway. She gave me a hug and whispered something I couldn't understand in my ear.

Later, I found out she lived on the same property as I did and everyone labeled her crazy. They assumed that because of the way she acted when she went around the neighborhood. She liked to drink beer and sometimes she would follow up with liquor, preferably gin, resulting her being drunk. She was drinking when I first met her on the bus stop, but not so much that she was staggering.

One day she came around and sat on my porch with some deep wounds that hadn't healed and asked me to pray for her. I did and she fell backward, then got up and praised God at the top of her voice. She didn't care who was listening and who thought she was crazy. She was thanking God and shouting out for Him to help her. I asked her what it was that made her draw toward me and she said without hesitation it was my smile. After praying for her, I invited her to go with me to church the following Sunday.

That morning, I didn't see her before I left, yet found out later that day she said she ran late, saw me drive off, and ran behind me trying to catch up but couldn't. Afterwards, she went with me almost every Sunday and even after I stopped going to that church, she continued as a member until the preacher became too demanding. Many people who knew her underestimated her because of her behavior. I looked past her outside and read her inside, which told a completely different story. She was intelligent, liked nice material things, liked to dress nice, loved God, really loved kids, and was smarter than others gave her credit. Most people would hide when they saw her coming. They didn't realize that this lady had gotten shot and had fragments and plates still lodged in her head. They didn't stop long enough to listen to her heart letting them know that quite possibly, that was the reason she acted like she did or drank like she did. They didn't give her the chance to hear her fear of darkness, staying up almost all night, crying out when beat up by her boyfriend, frightened when she heard sirens, and all of her other fears they wouldn't hear unless they stopped and listened. She went to doctors with no avail. Why wouldn't someone take time to tell her that the only answer she has is God? Oh yes, I forgot, she's crazy!

We need to stop calling or thinking that so-called "different than us" people are crazy just because their actions are not like ours. We are judging them not knowing the reasons behind their behaviors. We don't know what they're feeling inside because we are too judgmental of their outside. Sometimes the only thing a person needs is a hug to let them know that maybe one person in the whole world cares about them. If we think that we're too good for that small gesture, then we're the ones in trouble and not them. We feel like we're going to get something on our clothes or they may transfer over a disease to us, and if the truth is known, they are probably cleaner than us. One thing we have bad is to continue rubbing a person's sin consistently in their face either through mentioning it too much or demanding an immediate change. What we forget is those people already know they have the problem and reminding them daily only pushes them away from us. You cannot badger them about their sin because you can't heal that sin anyway, only God can. Your job is to get them to know, trust, and believe in God and allow Him to take it from there because only He knows every hurt that person hasn't told you about. If we could heal, we would only heal the surface, but when God heals, He will heal everything beneath. When she said it was my smile that led her to me, it really was Jesus who she saw in my smile letting her know it was fine to ask me for a hug. When I saw and got to know her, I knew someone long ago had planted a good seed in her just by the way she talked and her running to catch up so she could go to church. She was running to be in the presence of God and probably needed that peace. Satan was satisfied with her and the way people treated her before I came along because now, he has a challenge to hold onto her. He won't stop, but he has a fight on his hand and Jesus will win. Satan wants us to judge others, that way we'll stay away from them giving him an "open season" to prey on their weaknesses. He knows they're not strong enough in God to fight him, that's why God sends them our way. We have to stop running and hiding from them, yet stop and listen to their hearts.

Each day sitting on my porch, I would see this lady pass by going to work and also when she would be returning home. Each time we would speak and end our greetings with "God bless you" to each other. One morning sitting on my friend's porch, I spoke to this lady asking her how was she doing. She lifted her arms toward heaven and screamed that she wanted to be free as a bird. So again, we exchanged "God bless you" and she went back home. That same evening I was sitting on my porch, looked up after hearing someone screaming my name, and it was her running toward me, crying. I didn't really know her, but from her hurtful cries, I knew something was wrong. I took her inside my house and asked her what was wrong and she was very upset because a male stranger made a move on her and she still had open wounds from her previous husband. She had drank a few beers with a friend of hers and his advance brought back old memories she had tried to forget.

I told her I was going to pray for her and called in two female witnesses for help. One of those witnesses had gone through the same thing she was going through, so I gave them time to exchange notes before I prayed. After they talked, I anointed her and started praying over her combined with silent prayers from my two witnesses.

All of a sudden, this lady started shaking violently, screaming to God to help her, throwing up so much we had to get a garbage bag to catch it all, sweating, and then calming down with her eyes shut. Then she began to shake again and again. I started praying and rebuking those demons out of her. This went on for a while and suddenly, there was a peace upon her that I cannot describe. All we could do was praise and thank God for His work. This was the first time this had ever happened to me and it was like the little girl in the movie *The Exorcist* played out in real life. Her vomit was spewing out just like it was in the movie. It frightened me at first, but I was not going to let those demons win because I knew Jesus was in the midst and our prayers were stronger.

The next day she started stopping by the porch and getting a hug to and from work every day. Many times, she would come back and sit after she went home and changed clothes, wanting to hear more about this Jesus who was being discussed every day. After a while, she even started going to church and Bible study each week. She also introduced her friends to getting to know Jesus and would always praise Him in front of them for what He was doing in her life. She would ask lots of questions in Bible study simply because she wanted to understand fully so she could try to live in a godly way. She generously gave her free time to any function set up to help the ones needing help. Her boldness praising God was apparent around everyone, definitely not ashamed. She even exerted that same godly boldness when she was at work.

God knew when this lady and I were speaking to each other that she would need Him through me one day. All He was doing from the very first day we spoke was setting the stage. A smile and a greeting don't hurt anyone, yet may be the thing so preciously needed to a person who is hurting inside. I really didn't know what she wanted to be free of, nor did I give it anymore thought and for sure didn't know that same night God, through me, would give her that freedom. God was showing me then He was going to use me at His anointed time. God also set the stage that night with a witness who had just come through what this lady was going through and could minister to her letting her know she wasn't the only one. Satan knew she was weak and hurting because of her husband, so he sent that demon around her to reopen her wounds. What Satan didn't know was God had already set up someone she could run to and not even the beer drinking would stop her.

God knew her heart and answered her "freedom" prayer she had asked for that morning. Her vomiting was a sign of cleansing her insides of those demonic spirits and making her inside new. Those demons didn't want to come out of her, but God's power was too great and they had no choice. That's why when it was all over she had an indescribable peace glowing all over her. What God sets free, is free indeed. That is direct proof that when God is really involved, there has to be a change. God always looks past our faults and sees our needs. Jesus told the blind men not to go tell anybody, but they had to go and tell because they just couldn't hold His greatness to themselves. That's what happened to her after she was set free. She couldn't hold it in, yet boldly told people how great Jesus was. This led to her recruiting for Christ and persuading them to go to church and Bible study with her. She even took her Jesus message and attitude to work with her. When God brings us out of something, we need to tell somebody.

One day we were sitting on the porch as normal and suddenly, I heard someone to my right screaming out my name. I looked and saw this young single mother of one running over toward me holding onto her young daughter. When she approached the porch, she asked me if she could talk to me privately. I agreed to talk to her, invited her into my apartment, and sat down to discuss her problems. She told me that she had talked to others including this preacher, but nothing had happened. The first thing she told me was she was coming down from a drug high that she went on the day before. This was evening of the next day, so she said she hadn't slept since she went on this high. She strongly asked me not to repeat any of what she was about to tell me because she didn't want anyone to know her business. I told her that I would respect her wishes. She told me she had three problems that she didn't know what to do about or how to handle.

Her first problem was a rental company was going to repossess all of the furniture she was renting from them because of nonpayment. She said she had called them, offered them the small amount of money she had, but they refused to accept that partial payment. Her second problem was the energy company. It given her a current date for full payment or they were going to turn off her electricity. She said she didn't have the money, nor would any of her friends or family loan or give her the amount. She was horrified with this because of her child's welfare. Her third problem was that she wanted to look for a job and work, but couldn't because all of the day cares she sought didn't have any openings. She had to rely on the bus service because she had no transportation.

I then told her, even being in her drugged condition, that God still loved her and heard her cry for help. She said she knew it was wrong but just got caught up in the wrong environment with peer pressure. I told her the only one who could fix all of her problems was God because there's nothing too hard for God. Then I called in one female witness who was still sitting on my porch to pray with this girl and myself. During this prayer, you could definitely feel the precious presence of God. After the prayer, I gave her a hug and noticed she wasn't crying and normally most young people I pray for show that reaction, but she showed none. I knew God was there and told her I wanted her to go home, fall to her knees, ask God for forgiveness, ask God to come into her life as her personal Savior, and ask Him to help her.

Then, she got hold of her little girl and went back home. A little later, this girl came running back over to my apartment with excitement and asked again if I could talk to her. She said she didn't understand because as soon as she opened her door, she just started crying for no reason. She said she then fell on her knees, prayed to God still crying, and a feeling came over her she'd never felt before. She said she had never experienced that feeling when others had prayed or spoken to her. She also told me that when I was praying for her, she had felt this feeling in her chest that she had never felt before. I told her that she had just experienced the true presence of God and He was with her even in her mess. Then she hung around my apartment for a long time as though she had found perfect peace, then she returned home.

A day or two had passed and I hadn't seen or heard from her until seeing her pass by with the person she told me gave her the drugs. I knew then that she had relapsed. The next day she came back to me with this humble and embarrassed look asking to talk to me again. Right before she said a word, I told her that I knew she had used, but God would forgive her and He still loved her. She asked me to go to her apartment to talk to her and I agreed to go taking a witness with me.

When I got into her apartment, I denounced her nasty and messy living conditions telling her she needed to clean up without excuses. I also told her that God was a forgiving God and He would still answer her prayers. We began to talk about her wanting to put her daughter in daycare so she could work, but there was no opening. As soon as we finished talking about it, her cell phone rang and it was a daycare worker informing her they had an opening for her daughter. When she got off of the phone with a smile and told me the message, I told her in a praising behavior, “Do not tell me what my God can't do.” I told her to pray and thank God, then my witness and I left in overwhelmed joy.

A little later, my phone rang and it was her. She told me she had just got off of the phone with the rental company. The representative had agreed to accept the money she had offered earlier and they would work with her on the rest of the back payments. They told her they were not going to pick up the furniture. Again, I reminded her how great God was and for her to pray and thank Him.

A few minutes later, she called me again telling me that a relative who had always refused to lend her money called and agreed to pay her entire utility bill so she didn't have to worry. This overjoyed us. It was an awesome feeling when she told me that when she went to others, nothing happened, but when she came to me, things happened.

Weeks had passed and I hadn't seen this girl and unfortunately, she went back to her old ways so things weren't going good for her. There even was this rumor that she had lied that I had touched her inappropriately in a Bible study and a host of other untrue statements. I didn't know whether it was true or not, but I forgave her if she did, and allowed God to handle it.

Not too long afterwards, I was sitting on the porch and saw some black smoke coming from an unknown apartment. Something hit me when I noticed the area it was coming from was this girl's apartment. When the firefighters put the fire out in her apartment, that fire never touched any other apartment and each apartment is only separated by nothing but a thin wall. I knew then God had his hands in the midst of this situation.

Since then the girl disappeared and I'm unsure where she went. One thing I do know is that a seed was planted during my relation with her causing her to remember God's goodness. Hopefully that will be the reminder to redevelop a relationship with God and ask that He guide her in her walk.

When you walk with God, there's something special in you that attracts even strangers to you. When people come to us with their deepest hurts, they expect us to keep it confidential and not judge them. The Jesus in us gives them the trust they need knowing we can help without putting their business all in the streets. God sent her to me because she had done all she knew to do and had talked to others. When we've done all we can do, try Jesus. Satan deceives you with drugs, etc., making you so high you forget about your problems for a short while, but he never reveal that at a certain point, you have to come down and face the same old problems. For a lot of us that's an out we're willing to take over and over, yet never solving anything. In fact, our original problems seem to get worse each time we take advantage of each of our outs. Satan doesn't want you with a godly person and that's the reason he continues to put those ungodly counselors in front of you. He controls them so you think that drugs are the answer until he gets you hooked. Not only is he confusing your mind with the ups and downs from the drugs, but it's slowly wearing down your physical body. Satan doesn't care how you look as long as you keep serving him and when your body stops, he just goes to his next victim. That's the reason he keeps his likeness always coming back tempting you with your weakness. Even if you're strong in God, Satan will continue sending someone or something ungodly around you to tempt you into coming back to him. If he tried to tempt Jesus three times knowing who Jesus was, why wouldn't we think he would try our very weak minds? That's why we have to die and renew our strength through Christ daily so we can fight off anything trying to pull us away from God.

When the girl said there was a feeling she couldn't explain, when God is present in your midst, it is something you can't describe, but you know it's real. *If two or more come together in My Name, there I shall be also.* God knows we're not perfect and wouldn't we be in trouble if He were a one-time forgiver? Even we who claim or try to walk with Him will fall short of His expectations. He forgives us over and over because, unlike us, He holds no grudges. We also have to remember that nothing is too hard for God and nothing is impossible for God. Any door flesh closes and even locks, God can open and unlock. God made the one who closed or locked it in the first place and allowed the locks and doors to be made. God proves Himself through unlocking those doors to make us believe that He is a rewarder of those who diligently seek Him. After He opens them, it's then up to us to keep them open by not allowing Satan through those doors. If we continue to be disobedient to God, He will remove Himself from our situations and allow us to take a great fall. We develop the attitude we needed God to open the door, but now that we're in, we can keep it open. We forget we couldn't open or hold it open on our own the first time, so what makes us think this time will be any different? We certainly can't talk about or degrade the ones God used to allow Him to get us out of our mess. Always remember it was God who sent you to them in the first place. *Touch not my anointed nor do my prophet no harm.* Believe me, the wrath will be upon you if you do!

There was this guy who used to walk all around the property talking to people who weren't there. He always carried around this boom-box listening to loud music. Most people would just stare at him and were probably afraid to approach him being uncertain of his actions. He would even drive his mother's car, but she stopped that because it was too dangerous. When he did drive her car, he would stop at the top of the hill, gun the engine, then speed down the street without caution to anyone, not even the kids. I hardly ever saw him holding a conversation with anyone, yet always by himself. At one point, he would sleep in the property washhouse every night after, we guessed, his mother had put him out. At times, you would also see him appear to be fighting and cursing with the invisible.

After watching him, I concluded that this man was full of demons that had taken over his life. It was like he was afraid to come directly on the porch when we were out there talking about God. Rebuking his demons was a regular occurrence when we would approach or see him pass by. Each time we would rebuke them, his actions would react dramatically. If he was walking on the same side of the street facing us, as soon as he noticed us, he would cross to the other side getting as far away from us as possible. He would walk down the street in front of us with his music loud and as soon as we rebuke those demons, he would immediately turn the volume down. A few times when he was walking across the open field that was a good distance from us, we would rebuke the demons and he would look back and curse us. I knew from his reactions to our rebuking that he had some bad spirits controlling his life and he needed a big dose of Jesus. The only problem was he wouldn't allow us to get close enough to him. His actions would intensify when he was drinking alcoholic beverages.

I remember several times when I was on regular godly walks, I would stop by the corner store and he would literally wait outside until I would come out before he went in. It was like his demons didn't want to be under the same roof as a godly man.

These actions between the two of us went on for a long time until one day, while during my walk, I ran into him by the store. This time he didn't run from me, which was very shocking. He even started talking normally to me and that gave me a chance to minister to him and invite him to church. Even with the demonic spirits, you could still tell there was a seed planted in him from his earlier years. This was after allowing him to tell me about his drugs and women taking advantage of him. After our conversation, he went his way and I went mine. I didn't see him anymore for weeks and thought that he had left the property.

One Sunday at church on the property, a sister motioned for me to come to her as she pointed outside. I saw this demon-possessed man coming to church. He walked in and took a seat right beside me. All I could do was praise God because I hadn't seen him, nor did I tell him where the church was. As we were sitting there, he really got involved in the service, clapping his hands, and saying that was what he needed. This was an amazing blessing to have him in the presence of God. After service, he ate with us and held a conversation about his mother. He only came back once more and that was the last time, but was still walking around the property. At least we got a chance to water his seed to make it grow a little more and hope one day that growth will make him return to God wherever he is.

Demons and bad spirits are real whether we like to admit it or not. I believe those possessed see beings and things that normal fleshly eyes cannot see. We talk to God who is invisible to our eyes, yet we know His presence is there. Job talked to God because he wished God was human in his sight so he could plead his case. Those demon spirits that Jesus cast out of the two men into pigs were in the Bible. God will place even the worst in our paths just to see if we turn from them or are obedient and plant His Word in them. We have to listen first, then tell them what sayeth the Lord because He'll give you the words to say. Remember, God was the One who set up the meeting anyway.

It was direct proof when he found his way to the church unexpectedly, that God's Word doesn't come back void. God has the power over all spirits. When we met, the guy was hungry and thirsty in the spirit and had to search for a place where his spirit could feed on the Word and wash it down with the Holy Spirit. Sometimes we make an incorrect judgment assuming that some lost are too far gone and write them off without hearing their hearts. Satan wants to keep them confused and certainly doesn't want them near us at all. That's unfair because God uses us as His vessels to all, not just some. We don't realize that we could be in their place; how would we feel if vessels turned their backs on us? God even makes it easy for us by sending them to us and we don't even have to go looking for them. Jesus is not a respecter of man and we must try to walk as He did! Looking out of a fleshly eye, you would never think this guy would come close let alone go inside of a church. But that's how powerful the Word of God is and makes the demons shake all over.

A few months after we settled into our apartment and my son found something to do, he began coming home telling me this lady had him "pray before you play." Asking him what that meant, he told me that before they played, she would make all of them say a prayer. This had never happened to us before and I had to find out more about this lady. Then one day I was looking out of my bedroom window because there was something going on for the kids in the field between my apartment and the office. There was this lady sitting on a log that surrounded the bottom of this tree. She was talking to someone sitting with her and I noticed there was something different about her spirit. It was the way she moved her hand when she was trying to make her point to the person she was talking to. It was strange because out of all the people there, I couldn't get my eyes off of her.

Afterwards, I began to see her all of the time walking kids to and from school or just walking the property with some of her friends. Later, I found out this lady was in fact the one who would make my son pray before he played. I found that to be very impressive and finally got the opportunity to meet her. From the first time I met her, our spirits hit it off good. She was the first to start coming down to my apartment and sit with me on my porch. She had been in the complex longer, so she was able to give me inside information on what and who I was facing all around me, including history of the property during her stay. She really impressed me with her knowledge of the Bible and her love for Jesus. Her passion for kids was overwhelming and everywhere you saw this lady, you saw a bunch of kids following her. It was not done for her to look good, yet her love for each of them was genuine. She was one of the few I knew who would do without just to satisfy others' needs. She opened the door to her home to anyone who needed prayer, food, etc., which was admirable of her except she invited some bad spirits in the process. She gave everyone the benefit of doubt until they proved themselves different. Most times that would get her into trouble because they would prey on her goodness and use her for their own personal gain. She was unable to see lots of this misuse because of the kindness in her heart.

She would keep so many kids for so long, I would ask her if they had mothers. Many people judged her by the past she had left behind. God had given her a great talent of revelation so she could see the ones who judged her coming before they even got there. She had lots of enemies who perpetrated being her close friends. Her past developed a strong-willed woman and most times, Satan brought it back in trying to tempt her into physical confrontations. Many times God would reveal to her through a sign that something was about to happen. Many of those times God would place me in her presence before the problems would arise.

I told her on my first encounter with her and her enemies, just to let God handle all of her enemies. He would do it without her having to lift a finger, that He would make all of her enemies her footstools. All she had to do was sit, watch, and God would lay them down right in front of her. I even went as far as calling out the names and told her they would fall like dominoes.

The very next day after arguing with one and while sitting on my porch, this one got hit on the side of the head by another girl and had to come to my porch for assistance. She had to sit in the chair next to my friend and my friend was the one having to care for this same girl who earlier confronted her. These enemies of hers started dropping like flies, either through evictions, law violations, drugs, etc., whatever was necessary to leave the property. She was very outspoken about her beliefs and interpretations, which turned lots of so-called Christians against her. She would want to debate issues, but most of them would not give her their time of day. She was even told to go to some other Bible study because she was raising too many questions that they didn't care to take time to answer.

One of her biggest problems was putting her fleshly caring before obedience to God. God showed her three or more times that she shouldn't wrap her arms around this spirit. Each of those times this spirit was riding with her and God shut her car down. One of those times, the car had started earlier that morning and as soon as this spirit got in the car, the car refused to start. The worst part of all of these times was each time the car stopped, this spirit vanished out of sight not even trying to help get it started. Not only did my friend not heed to those warnings, she allowed this spirit to move in with her and her kids. She did it because this spirit had nowhere else, she said, to go. My friend thought everything was going good but the thing she forgot about were the signs God had showed her. All of a sudden, she began to coddle and make excuses for this spirit, inviting other like spirits around.

My friend's mind was totally deceived and was blind by all of the bad things that were surrounding her. All of a sudden, she was being taken from a comfort zone where God had her, to a hell where Satan wanted her, which she couldn't see coming. A house divided cannot stand. Her only way out was to clean out/around her house and hope

God would have mercy on her for being disobedient. God had placed her in a position where she could stretch her income to pay all of her bills each month. She had more than enough food each month to supply her family's needs, enough gasoline for her car to run, and even left her a little money to take her kids for a little fun time. God even made a phone company change its due date policy to correspond to her income date, which most companies would never do.

I knew this friend was going to be placed into my life because before I ever met her, I drew an image of her that I had seen in the cement of my porch. This was witnessed by a guy who was sitting with me at the time the image appeared. It happened the same as it did with my friend Joe. I knew that God placed her into my life because of our immediate closeness shared when we first met. We were totally opposite and the most obvious thing we had in common was God. I firmly believe that God knew we needed each other, because where one is weak, the other one is strong. God allows us to read the hearts and spirits of people by their actions, how they talk, and what they are saying. Good spirits shine like turning on a light into darkness because they echo a peaceful and inviting glow all around them.

When I saw my friend sitting under that tree, I believe God was showing me she was a seed of good fruit. God used my son's statements to make me become so curious it made me want to meet her. God will use anyone or anything to make sure His plan is fulfilled. Just with her words, I could tell that Jesus was residing in her. You don't have to prove yourself by boasting you can memorize. That motive is to make you look good. People will use your kindness as your weakness prompting Satan to exploit that weakness and make bad spirits seem like your closest friends. It's fine to be kind and generous, but be very careful not to get used. Pray to God to expose those ones with motives to use you, but at the same time, forgive them when they are revealed. God will show us early warnings that it's about to happen, but allows us to make the choice. Most times we don't heed His warnings and suffer the consequences later. Even with our enemies, we think we have to get physical and curse just to make the point of defense. God is our only defense we need because He said He'd make our enemies our footstools. He said, greater is he that's in us, than he that's in the world. He places a hedge of protection around us. The battle is not yours, it's the Lord. What part of His promises do we not get? If He said it, it's done and all we have to do is sit back, wait, and watch.

We have to be very careful how we treat God's people whom He has chosen to use. Mistreatment triggers God's wrath and that's what all of my so-called friends and enemies felt. *Touch not my anointed or do my prophet no harm!* Words of the Bible are not debatable, but man's interpretation may be. How can you ask someone to leave a supposed assembly of God just because they ask a few questions? If God is really there, He'll give all answers to all questions. Any question deserves an answer, especially a biblical one. The reason we don't answer or want to debate is that we think we know more than what we actually do (perpetrating) or we have an ego problem not wanting anyone to take center stage away. No one knows everything but God no matter how many manmade degrees you have hanging on your walls. Too many times we place ourselves on the level or above God. We as Christians have to be obedient to God even if the price tag is sacrifice. Each time we are disobedient, that opens up a door for Satan to walk through. We then make a fleshly decision that our way is better than God's way. Doing it our way results in un-seeable mistakes being made instead of relying on God.

Satan knows this and as soon as we make our first mistake, he moves in. He's going to make you think that the past you've overcome doesn't look so bad and those desires were easier to get. Long suffering with a blessed eternal end is much better than non-suffering with a quick end. A future with Satan is like a cube of ice, it's solid for a while but slowly melts back to water. Many times we get in God's way with us trying to help our brothers or sisters. He gives us signs beforehand to feed them with His Word. Instead of being obedient to God's wishes and overlooking the signs, we give them exactly what they don't need at the time. We try to play God and do His job, but all we're doing is interfering in His plan.

God will even put vessels in our path to confirm His signs, remind us of the disobedient consequences, and instruct us to step back, yet we don't. God may have the ones we want to help in that situation to fall deep so the only one they can call on is Him.

God won't punish us because we want to help our neighbor, yet because of our disobedience to Him, especially after ignoring His warning signs. Many times God knows that the only way to help that person is to take away all excuses except calling on His Name. If this is a bad spirit that you invite into your house, then that spirit will invite other bad spirits in. All of a sudden, it will get so bad and confusing, you sit back wondering what happened. At this point all you can do is thoroughly clean out your house and pray. As long as those bad spirits are around, they know exactly what turns you on and just how you like it.

The only reason the first bad spirit wants to invite the other bad spirits is to keep you so satisfied preying on your weakness each day, that you just desire more and more. After a while, you're surrounded both day and night with nothing but these bad spirits that keep coming like their on shifts. That way you won't have time to call on God or even want to call on God. This will keep on until you find yourself back in the same past that God brought you out of. You stop caring about everyone and everything that used to mean something to you. Then, all of a sudden, everything you touch doesn't work and continues with no end in sight. The bad things start to happen one by one and back to back not giving you time to fix the first before the next one hits you. Confusion is everywhere and that's exactly where Satan wants you. Satan doesn't want you to have room to think because he's afraid that you may remember who brought you out of your mess the last time. He knows he'll lose if he allows you enough space to call upon God to help you. Although all of the above is going on, God is still watching. He'll put people in our lives that will maybe tell us something we don't want to hear or something that may not feel too good to us at the time, but it sticks with us. They may not be necessarily the ones we would fleshly pick, but God knows what we need and will use the best spirit to give us His message. When God allows us to go through things without allowing us to be killed in the process and brings us out, He already has someone He'll send our way. He wants that one to know even when there seems no hope in his situations, God is the hope and he will respond to Him bringing us out. If we don't personally go through things ourselves, how can we answer or guide others through the most detailed hurts they're facing and/or going to face?

There have been many others whose lives God has touched when they stopped by my porch. I know that God had anointed my porch because it drew all kinds of lost and saved souls to it. Many of them wouldn't understand, but they said it was something that made them come and sit on the porch. You could tell the ones Satan had totally caught up because they would rush by without even touching the cement. The ones that did step onto the cement couldn't stay very long, especially when the Word began. But, even with them, I know the words they heard planted or watered a seed. There have been so many that it's impossible to record them all, even though I remember them all. I don't know some of their endings, but my only job was to water their seed when they stopped by, and let God handle the rest. God just sent them by for a little while to give them just enough to get the next stage where He wanted them.

We cannot allow ourselves to feel bad, think we could've or should've done more, feel we should've spent more time, or any other negatives after they are gone. God showed you what to do and told you what He wanted you to say on their brief stop and if He would've wanted more out of you, it would've happened. Stop thinking you can put them on your back and piggyback them with you up to Heaven. Only they and God can get them to Heaven no matter how long you stay with them, that isn't our decision. Just be blessed that God chose you for them to spend some of their brief time with on their way to wherever He's taking them. My porch was and is a ministry in itself.

There was one Christian lady that labeled it the Porch Ministry because she personally experienced the peace and anointing that's there. Below are just a few whom God sent by and had to stop for a brief time.

There was this guy who had to travel by wheelchair because of his physical condition. He was a total stranger to me. The first time I met him was when I was on my way home and he was rolling himself up a hill going to the corner store. We spoke and he passed on by, but there was something telling me to go back and push him up the hill the rest of the way. When I got to him and introduced myself, I told him God told me to push him the rest of the way. He declined my offer stating that doing it himself was the way he got his exercise. When I told him that I had to because I had to be obedient to God, he allowed me. There was not very much conversation between us, but he thanked me after we reached the store. After that incident, I would see him here and there but we hardly ever stopped and talked. I knew God had put him in my path for some reason but I didn't know why.

One day while sitting on the porch, he wheeled himself up to the curb in front of the porch. When I saw him, I went to him and when I got there he told me he just had to come over to talk to me. He then said that he was writing rap music about the world, but the rap would always turn over into a spiritual rap and he didn't understand why. I told him that God was the one who gave him the talent and He was trying to tell him to use the talent for God's will. I told him that he could go with his world rap, but sooner or later it would end, but if he obeyed God going with a spiritual rap, it would last forever. He told me that he understood and we talked a little further about Jesus, then he left.

God sent him by there to get the right interpretation of his confusion.

There was this other guy that used to drive by going to his friend's apartment to drink beer with him. Each time he would drive by, he would look over to the porch and point at me, then wave. It was like he'd have to turn his head toward the porch every time he passed by. He acted like he was always happy but something told me he had some problems he was trying to hide in his beer drinking.

One day he was passing by, I stopped him, and introduced myself to him. Afterwards, he just continued passing by pointing and waving at me. One day he was passing by and just as I expected him to wave, he stopped in front of my apartment. I walked out to his truck and found him in a bad emotional shape. He said it was the first time that he and his wife had fought as bad as they did. We talked about his problem allowing him to mainly get it off of his chest and afterwards, he thanked me for being there when he needed someone. God had shown him such a peace exhibited on the porch and in me, that he felt he could trust me with such an intimate part of his life. He really wasn't trusting in me, yet it was the Jesus living in me because I was a stranger to him. Afterward, he continued coming by but instead of just pointing and waving, he would stop each time and fellowship with us. He felt safe on the porch because no one judged him and we welcomed him with open arms. He got prayed for, enjoyed talking about Jesus, received biblical answers he had longed questioned, and after a while, began to replace his friend's visits for sitting on the porch. This porch became his refuge and he started leaving his beer in his truck.

One day I was sitting out on the porch and a property maintenance man came by and asked me if he could come back by after he got off from work to talk to me. I agreed to speak with him and after he got off, he came over. I had already seen the tension among all of the workers, especially the one who has been on property the longest, and they had made the one I was to talk to the supervisor. There's a big difference when you are just one of the workers and suddenly you are their supervisor, especially with the ones who thought they should've gotten that promotion. He began to tell me of the problems he was having with his marriage, then the problems God had already revealed he was having at work. I told him that God would fix his marriage and give him all new workers if he trusted Him. Then I prayed for him. A while later, I asked him how his marriage was going and he told me they were really working at it and it was getting better. When his wife and daughter would come to pick him up from work, you could sense this family peace atmosphere between all of them. I knew then their marriage had gotten better and God was the key to unlocking that door. Then later, all of a sudden, the property management began to transfer out all of the older workers, bringing in new ones. After all was said and done, this supervisor had gotten a completely new crew working under him. God had not only restructured his family, but He also restructured his work environment, all for the better.

One thing we must remember after God blesses us with our desires, we must not stop praising and worshiping Him. It seems sometimes after things begin to go right for us, we forget about God and act like we don't need Him anymore. We tend to feel like now we can do the rest on our own, which is far from the truth. When we're down, we cry, call out His name, and any other behavior we know to get God to hear us. When things seem to be going good, He never hears from us. Now it's up to this supervisor to stay with God so both of his blessings will last, but if not, he'll end up in the same old place or worse.

There was this other maintenance worker who worked on property. He knew and served God. At first we would just wave and speak, but a little later, the anointing of the porch drew him to it also. He became a regular on the porch, both during and after working hours. Even when he was on duty on the weekends, he would come over to the porch wasting time until his next call. He didn't want to chance driving back the long journey home if he had to just turn right back around and drive back. We would always just sit and talk about the Lord relating our talks with current world events. We would talk about his family, church, and his work, giving off the expression that he had a personal relationship with God.

One day he asked me if he could stop by and talk to me

about a problem he had encountered on the job. He confided in me that this female resident had filed a sexual complaint against him while he was repairing her apartment and it wasn't true. He allowed me to pray for him on that issue and more because he knew that God was his only answer. After I prayed for him outside on the porch, he gave me a hug and began to stumble to his vehicle. He said that was the first time that had happened to him and he expressed this relieving peaceful smile. I knew then that God had His hands on the worker and everything would be fine. Now, this guy was about six feet tall weighing over 200 pounds and to see him stumbling from the presence of God was amazing. The peaceful smile he had on his face was a reflection of relief to know everything would be fine. It's amazing how God set the stage with just a wave or a greeting, then, draws you in like a magnet. God knew long ago that I needed to be on my porch at that specific time to receive this worker.

As long as Satan is traveling to and fro trying to get us on his team, we are going to be tested. Satan doesn't like it when two true Christians come together and discuss the Lord because he knows that Jesus is in the midst. He knows we will tell him to "get thee behind us" sending him to go bother someone else. A little while after, this guy was moved to another property but I'm not worried as long as he keeps on his full armor and continues trusting God to fight his battles.

When I was staying with my stepdaughter for a week, I

used to pass by this guy's apartment every day. He most times would be sitting out on his porch alone watching the traffic. There was something about him that would always stick with me that I couldn't figure out because he would hold his head down most times. It was as if something was troubling him most of the times I would pass by. I would see him sometimes walk to the store or around the complex grounds and he would always again have his head down.

One day I finally met him, noticing that his hands were shaking uncontrollably, and invited him to go to church with me. He told me he could go every other Sunday because of his obligation to another ministry and I accepted that. At that time I didn't want to pry into his problems, but hoped that he would offer them to me himself. He started going to church with me and began to sit out on the porch with me every day from morning until afternoon. The first thing I noticed was that he had a set time for everything he had to do because he kept asking me what time it was. If we were talking and his time was up in the afternoon, he would immediately get up and leave. He had a certain time he would knock on my door, go eat lunch, fix his dinner, and go to bed allowing nothing to interfere. Then he began to walk with me on my routes with God and found great satisfaction in them because he was learning more about the One we served. He began to confide in me his most intimate parts of his life, including his illness. He started sticking to me like glue finding out he was paranoid when he would sit in his apartment too long. He was scared of people knocking on his door after 7 p.m. His problem was so bad that he had to get home before it got dark and he would always leave my apartment around 2 p.m. precisely.

One day we started talking about our old days when we were getting drunk and running the clubs. We started bringing up names of the people we used to hang with during those times and, surprisingly, found out that we knew each other and used to hang out together. We knew we remembered each other's faces, but didn't know how each was so familiar. Back in those days, we weren't close friends, but we were close acquaintances and knowing this strengthened our current relationship.

God sometimes shows us people and initially we have no idea why we keep running into them or why we remember their faces. Even if we see the hurts or problems, we greet them and pass them by because of being careful of intruding into someone else's problems. History has shown us that many people don't want anyone else in their problems or hurts and we have to respect their wishes. The only one who can invite us in at their request or God's request is God. God knows their hurts and problems, chooses who to send His lambs to, and will orchestrate the meetings. We may pass each other by many times, but the meeting will only happen when God is ready because He has to give us the words to say. If you run into a person and continue to run into that person, it could be that God, maybe not immediately, will connect you together at a later date. This is exactly what happened to my friend and me. God knew what he needed and knew that I would understand the patience it would take for him to overcome his problems. When he started walking with me, he would get tired, but later walks would become much easier. He got to the point that he would look forward to them because the walks were helping him physically and mentally. He began to get less paranoid and would stay out later, even after night had fallen. He didn't need a doctor, just a belief in God and giving Him all of the praise. I prayed for him but I couldn't heal him, God had to make that happen. It was so ironic that we were together serving the devil and for God to put us back together to serve Him. What would be the chance after all of those years, man could do that? God knew even back when we both were running the streets together that we would meet each other again living in the same complex. God knows the beginning and the ending of each one of our lives, no coincidence yet His will.

There was this almost blind man whom I would always see walking past the porch. Sometimes I would see him with his cane and sometimes I would see him without. I found out later that he was blind in one eye and almost blind in the other eye, but he had refused to allow his handicap to keep him from living a normal life. He also refused to let it dictate what he was or wasn't going to do, nor was he going to feel sorry for himself or allow others to do so. You could tell he was searching for the missing piece in his life not really knowing what it was. We began to speak at first as we passed each other, then as time went by, we began to talk more and more. Then each Sunday I would run into him at our church on property and he would always be sitting on the front row. I realized then what he was missing in his life. Our relationship had gotten to the point that every time he would see me, he wanted me to give him a hug as though that got him ready for whatever he was going to face.

One day he introduced his wife to me and she was very charming. She seemed to be a perfect match for him. I invited her to church because he was the only one I would see there, but she said she couldn't be around a lot of people in a closed environment. Something must have changed her mind because the following Sunday she was there. I left the church on property because of a confused environment, but they stayed for a couple more Sundays, then quit going. He said the reason they left was because he didn't feel that special feeling he felt when we preached at the church. They were also drawn to the porch when they would wait for the bus or just stop on their way to the store. We developed this very special relationship that remains close even as of this writing. We walk past so many people who need and are searching for Jesus, but we allow their handicaps or illnesses to overshadow their real needs. Sometimes we are so selfish in our own healthy bodies that we take for granted that others don't have the same privileges. We never think that we could ever be in those same positions. We must always remember that they have feelings and souls too and again, it's not his/her outside appearance but their insides. Everyone needs a personal relationship with God, no matter what their physical defects are and God loves them no less. When he needed the hug from me, it was not me that he needed the hug from, it was Jesus through me. That hug told him that he could make it and everything would be fine. Not only did God draw my friend close to Him but also drew his wife. Confusion is of Satan and when it is in a church, the people won't stay, even if they are babies in Christ. Also, they won't stay if they feel the same when they leave as they did when they came in. The presence of God brings changes and peace, therefore, no matter how well you fake it, everyone will know the difference. If I never see them again, I know they carry a seed that has been watered and any bad they encounter will be handled by God. His blindness may show a lot of darkness, but his heart does show lots of light.

There was this young man who had a young friend that was going through things she couldn't handle. The two were on their way to the store, but detoured around to my porch. The young man said that he didn't understand why they didn't keep straight because it would've been easier to go directly to the store. He said it was like something guided them across the lots knowing it was the long way to the store. When they got here, he asked me if I could talk to his friend and maybe I could help her with her problems. I agreed and invited her into my apartment to explain what was weighing her burdens down. She told me of all her problems and told me she didn't know where to turn. After we finished with our discussions and telling her she needed Jesus to fix her problems, I asked her if I could pray for her. She agreed and I invited her friend, son, and my witness to join us in my apartment. We circled around holding hands and after I anointed her with oil, I prayed for her. After asking Jesus to join us, the Holy Spirit came down so strong, it was evident His presence was there. All who were circled holding hands began to tremble because God had come down so strong and bold. The girl I was praying for started to tremble and cry, getting all of that old out making room for the new.

After we went back out on my porch, her smile told the whole story. I see her every so often and she's still smiling, telling me everything is still going good for her. When we're hurting, God will use others to guide us to His vessels so they can help us. He will also switch our routes without us knowing why, yet allow us to understand later. We will be going one way and in an instant, change our minds to go another way having unclear reasons. Her friend knew of me through one of the ladies who sits on my porch and God guided him to the place where she could get help.

Many people think that their world has ended and just give up hoping for the best, but they don't know all they have to do is call upon the Lord. The same God that heard

His people crying out when they were captured and held by Pharaoh, is the same God we are serving today that hear our cries. He will also send us a Moses to rescue us in our times of need.

She was crying out and nobody heard her but God, then He sent her friend (Moses) to guide her out of her Egypt. Can you imagine the joy felt after they went through the Red Sea, then, see the waters flow back down swallowing up their enemies? That has to be how this girl felt after crying out her hurts and realizing there is a promising future ahead for her. God wants us to cast all of our problems on Him so He can give us rest. Call on the Lord and He will come.

One day my neighbor came over telling me she has this friend who needed me and asked me if I could speak with her. She informed me that her friend had said that she didn't believe in God anymore. My neighbor was told this by her friend when she was trying to tell her friend about the goodness of God. I agreed to speak with her and told my neighbor to send her over to me. So when she came over, she had her friend to come and sit with us on my porch. I didn't realize it at first, but a little later, I figured out she and her friend were a gay couple. I began by asking her to tell me about her problems and initially she hesitated, but then began to talk. Her first words were her not believing in God because He hadn't done anything for her because of the bad position she was in. She was really blaming God, feeling that He wouldn't have let her get into her awful position, especially if He was real. She had served time in prison and she thought the world and God were totally against her because nothing positive was happening in her life. She was a mother to this little girl and exposing her to the gay lifestyle she was living. How did she expect things to go right when she was silently teaching an innocent child a lifestyle that is totally not of God? She went on saying that the only peace she had in prison was when this lady would come in each week or month and tell her about the Bible and God. She continued by saying that as soon as she began to trust and believe, something else would happen and she would get into trouble again. She said that she would even see black images on the walls and ceilings at night keeping her from going to sleep.

She said that when she got out of prison, things still didn't go right for her so she forgot about God. It was a few of us on the porch and I asked her if I could pray for her. You could tell her mate, even though she was talking a little, didn't like what was going on, but it was nothing she could do with our breakthrough. I asked God to come down, show His presence when I prayed and His Spirit came down with such a forceful realness, there was no doubt He was there. This girl cried and cried, having no control over her behavior. She even went and sat in her vehicle alone after we all hugged, then cried some more. She then accepted and believed that God was real, that it was going to take an effort on her part to change her life around. We invited them to church and to start fellowshipping with us, which they agreed. They started going to tent meetings, church, etc., with us on a regular basis, showing promise. We would bless them with school supplies, clothes, gas money, food, shoes for her daughter, etc., anything we could just to help them get on their feet.

All of a sudden, their promises turned to lies and they stopped coming around. Right before they had completely stopped coming around, you could tell that Satan was moving into their lives through her other mate. She was the most dominant one in that relationship and kept her away from us because she was losing control. She preyed on her weakness knowing that she wouldn't get spiritually refueled if she kept her from coming around us. Since then and up until this writing, I haven't seen or heard from either of them, but knowing it's God's purpose in His plan. I knew going in that this would be a little challenge because of her lifestyle and disbelief in God, but I also knew that I was going to win. I knew that when God's Word goes out, it doesn't come back void and that God would give me the words to say to her. He knew her condition much better than me and also how deeply her hurts went. I couldn't judge her because she led a gay lifestyle because that wasn't my job. God loved her as much as He loved me, He just didn't love her sin. We forget the lost are humans made in God's image also and they hurt like we do. They just allowed man to change their minds toward their original images to a sexual fakeness.

We were fortunate enough we got out of some of our sins, but they have no idea how to get out of theirs. We must not allow ourselves to get caught up into our feelings about someone's bad habits because God is the only one who can change them anyway. We need to stop thinking that we're God. They come to us because they have no other place to go and if we initially are critical of their outside, they'll never trust us with their inside. We need to have a blank mind and allow them to cry out about whatever's troubling them. Initially, if they don't mention their gayness or whatever it might be, we must not mention or spiritually beat them down against their sin. Remember, they are beginning to be a baby in Christ and we have to take one step at a time. They already know what their sins are and we don't need to pour salt into an open wound. They've already taken enough bashing from others in Christ and out of Christ and they don't need that from the one who maybe can lead them the right way. Believe me, they can sense the ones they can't trust. When people blame God for their bad positions, they're just making excuses because deep down they know it was the bad decisions they've made. They also realize they don't know how to correct those decisions and don't want to ask because of initial judgments. It's easier for them to place blame elsewhere. When they say God hasn't done anything for them, we must not get angry with them because we know they are spiritually ignorant and we know better. We need to ask them what have they done for

Jesus lately, then, explain that it was God who woke them up to even have the conversation they're having, not them. Also let them know even with them not believing God was alive, He still loves them enough to wake them up. The world only owes us a chance, but the chance/choice is up to us. If God isn't leading us, we will always make the wrong choices because we're leaning on our own understanding. Let's face it, we don't know our future, yet God does, so who should we allow to make our decisions? If we totally allow God to make our decisions, He will block the bad ones we face.

Those are some of the things God through me had to convince her of. Satan had deceived her enough to believe her lifestyle was fine and acceptable, even around her small daughter. God will send someone to introduce or reintroduce us to His Grace if He knows we're confused, but we must be patient. Sometimes it's a process and most of us want changes immediately. When we forget about God, it gives Satan an open door to have his way with us. Satan will put things that look good in front of us and make us believe that's the easy way out. Satan knows we're not spiritually strong enough to resist those temptations. In her case, Satan didn't want the other mate to get too involved because he already knew he was losing one lamb with the first girl. Satan knew he could use the unsaved one in the future to pull the saved one to her level when the saved one slipped again. Satan knew if he could keep her away from constant feeding from us, he had a better chance of holding onto her. What Satan doesn't know is that one day she's going to get hungry for some real spiritual food and his food won't satisfy her. Once you get a taste of God's goodness, you'll always have to go back for more because none can prepare it like God. She will lose her appetite, even for that lifestyle. Satan doesn't know her limit, but God does and when she reaches it, she'll change, leaving everything of Satan behind her. When she does come out, God will use her to tell her story to someone else because she'll know that the only one who brought her out was God. I claim that in the name of Jesus.

D: PLAYING WITH GOD

Some people just don't understand or get it. It is very dangerous to perpetrate in the name of God. They may fool some people, but they can't fool God and He is the only One who counts. Almost anyone can read and memorize the Bible, but does that make them of God or of themselves? Real children of God don't have to perpetrate because they will automatically stand out from all others. There will be something different in their smile, handshake, wave, eyes, etc., any demeanor making others comfortable and safe with them. How can you tell lost lambs how good Jesus is if you're high on drugs, drunk, etc., while you're telling them? Most people who are perpetrating will start their conversations reciting scriptures, bragging on how God is telling them this or that, trying to make you think they are perfect in God, bragging on how many Christian TV shows they look at daily, anything that comes to their minds trying to prove they are real Christians. Most times these people have something to hide, feel inferior within themselves, and have hidden agendas. Lost lambs are very vulnerable and can be easily deceived by others' selfish actions. They don't care if they're leading those lambs into a ditch as long as they, not God, get the praise. The blind lead the blind into a ditch because neither really has eyes open to God. They'll brag about the spiritual music they listen to at home and in their vehicles all day. This is nothing but a front hoping that they are not exposed to their real selves. These fakes always want to pray for someone lost and don't understand their prayers are going no further than their lips. How can they lift someone up if they are still on the worldly ground? They always are quick to bring out their oil to anoint someone not understanding that it's not the oil, but your true belief that God is using you. They might as well save the oil and cook with it, for the good it's doing them. When the oil is just thrown in a drawer it is not blessed, anointed, or respected. It should be as holy as your vows with God because of your belief in both.

These people will perpetrate so long they will honestly believe in themselves, their practices (reprobated minds) and God will remove His hands from them. They will get away with it for a while, but sooner or later, even the unsaved will cast doubt on them. Even after they are exposed, they still try to make others believe in them and their practices. One of the major problems is that they hurt more and scatter those that originally believed in them. They make those lost souls mistrust the real and God-filled Christians who try to help them. These practices are really bad when the preachers take part in the hurtful outcomes. *Woe unto the shepherds who scatter my sheep!* The results or wrath for these actions are devastating. All of a sudden things began to happen to them they can't explain or don't want to own up to. They wonder what happened when things were going good, in their minds, and instantly, they began to go down hill. Everything they do to slow down or stop the slide doesn't work. Their physical bodies all of a sudden begin to develop twisting of half their faces, boils infiltrate their skin, they get hurts where they never had before, they lose sight in one or both eyes, bad diseases begin to make homes in their bodies, etc., almost any areas to let them know they can't use God's name in vain. Their finances begin to crumble, vehicles begin to stop, friends begin to stop coming around or answering their phones, jobs are replaced by others, kids get into trouble, etc. Every monetary thing lets them know they cannot lead God's lost sheep away from Him. God is the only One who can fix the wrath He's placed on them and even if they ask for and are given forgiveness, they still have to answer for their bad deeds. It's better if those people would stay in the world and continue serving Satan, rather than perpetrate and play with God. There are too many hurt souls that get affected, not just the perpetrator. It's better if you don't know or are ignorant of God's laws than to know and not follow them. Perpetrators normally want others to look up to them as their gods and not teach them they are on the same level as they are, serving one God. They make them feel like they have to go through them to pray, repent, etc., or God won't answer them. They make them feel like they don't have a direct line to Jesus themselves. God will hear the lost souls and their cries quicker than He will the voices of the perpetrators. Self is the perpetrator's best friend, not Jesus because everything has to evolve around them. Perpetrators brag a lot on their material things because that gives them a crutch to hide their own inferior truths. It makes them feel they have the right to demean the less fortunate because they're fearful of the challenge they'd face with others of same or higher ranks as them. They are really uncomfortable being in the company of higher ranks because they are scared they'll say the wrong thing or will not fit in. They feel more comfortable with ones they can control totally and restrain those who they fear are smart enough to take over their dominion. Perpetrators try to get close to top figures by conning them with humbleness just so they can get where they want to go. They play politics and are not smart enough to realize it. If they are in a setting, they want to be the center of attention, being the first to answer questions, the first to agree to pray, the first to volunteer to read scriptures, etc. They try to project how much they know about the Bible. They feel they gain respect by doing these things, yet later on, go back to their worldly behaviors and sins. They try to hide those bad behaviors, but God always puts someone around to see them. I ran into many perpetrators in the short time I'd been at my apartment, but all of them were revealed and none of them lasted.

E. "CHURCH IN THE HILL" WITH SATAN

Before I left the church I was going to, I noticed this lady in this open field on property having church service. Even if the weather was bad, she was still outside having church. She had a homemade rack pulpit, some chairs, and a very small sound system that were placed under a tent. She was spreading the true word to all who would listen counting on God's Word not coming back void. There would only be two or three each Sunday who would sit underneath the tree, but that didn't matter to her. If there was only one she could get to try Jesus, it would be well worth it to her. If there were one hundred sheep and one got lost, you would corral the ninety-nine and go look for the lost one. When you finally find the lost one, that one will mean more to you than the rest because the ninety-nine had each other and the one only had you to depend on. Not only that, one saved will produce a multitude. When I heard this lady, I knew from her spirit she was a sure child of God.

After I met her, she asked me to help her put up some tents because of a week-long revival she was having. I agreed and she also asked me to speak one night, which I also agreed. After the pastor of the church I was attending heard about my speaking engagement, he got upset because she didn't ask him first. Understanding the church's authority, he was really mad because I was asked and he wasn't. Also, he had badly talked about her and her ministry earlier and had the opportunity to be invited to speak, but declined because that little ministry was beneath him. He wanted to be the center of attention.

The night I spoke he had gotten dressed up and attended, but showed strong jealousy by not acknowledging the spirit that was there. He was also jealous because he had said he was going to do something for the neighborhood, yet never did, but she did. When we were stacking the chairs on the last night in the poolroom, I told the guy helping me that the poolroom was the place for the property church. A week or two later, I left the church I was going to and helped this lady start building this church on the property. She said God had given her a vision of the church and knew, even before she met me, that God had me gathering the people for the church. God gave us the name of "Church in the Hill" and we made an order of service. Many of the people from the neighborhood scheduled themselves to cook a dinner each week so we could feed after the services ended. It was so amazing because everyone wanted to participate and we had a long list that would last for weeks.

I began inviting people to attend and the interest was fantastic. We even had people off property talking about our church, not mentioning all of the ones on property. There were lost ones on property who asked me to come by their apartments and wake them up each Sunday morning so they could attend. I followed their requests and would always get a good response. We also started getting off-property followers coming to our church. The lady was so overwhelmed because she said God had given her the vision of feeding the people after church a long time earlier. Finally, we set up the church and had our first service. Many people mix up the church with the church house not realizing the people are the church. *Upon this rock I will build my church and the gates of hell shall not prevail in it.* This was the goal this sister and I had about this church on property. Going to church doesn't get you into heaven and there are many who are deceived in thinking that. Sure we are to assemble, but that doesn't mean always in a house because we are to lift up His name everywhere we are. Going to the church building just for the sake of making you or someone else note that you went is the wrong reason or motive. Many of our churches are fixed on the numbers for financial reasons instead of being fixed on the number of souls that are brought to Jesus. One soul to know Jesus is worth all of the money in the world because that one is your multiplication starter. If churches are centered on lifting up Jesus to the one soul who showed up, Jesus not only will send more souls, He'll supply all of their needs. We allow flesh to center our thoughts and forget all of the promises God made to us. If history is known about the large and successful churches, they started with a true belief that God would fulfill His promises when they had nothing but faith to hold on to. It's when God grows them to an extraordinary level that they begin to forget how they got there. They begin to allow greed to become their weakness and that's when Satan marches in making them forget about the souls. They begin to exercise all of their efforts on being like or being better than the other large churches instead of allowing God to take them where He wants them to go. God will remove His hands off of churches when they become more commercial than Him and also from those pastors and bishops who have an "I did it myself" attitude. They were giving God all of the glory when they had nothing and growing, then after getting big enough, they stole the glory from God for themselves. Then they shape all of their ministers, deacons, etc., who are under their authorities in their own image instead of God's image, making them their cronies. These people are mostly the ones in the church with direct connection with the lost souls, yet their copied "too good image" and "clock managed time" still don't express the godly conversations the lost souls need.

Jesus picked the ordinary to walk with Him as disciples and always was out with the lost souls. Many of the bishops and preachers get too high and mighty to go out with a sincere heart to reach those crackheads, drunks, filthily dressed, homeless, etc., forgetting where they or their most prestigious church members came from. If they do, they're doing it for fake reasons or selfish motives, none of which pleases God. Visions are something God gives us for His future purpose, yet sometimes we get confused thinking it was God when really it was our own satisfaction. If God gives us the vision, He'll give us everything we need, set the stage, remove any obstacles, and guide us to fulfillment. If He doesn't and it's our vision, there will always be problems and most times, we'll never reach our goal, especially using God as the front guy for our own selfishness. If we think God told us, and things aren't working, we need to question if God really told us to build that church, have that revival, etc., because things work when God is really involved. All through the Bible when Jesus walked the earth, He attracted people from all over, no matter where He went. If we claim Jesus is within us, it should be the same thing and if not, we need to question ourselves. Many times we want something so bad in our lives, we substitute our own voice for Jesus' voice.

We began our services each Sunday morning and because we had three people to bring the message, we decided to rotate each Sunday. There was a pastor who had a bread ministry on property, the sister, and myself who all thought were on the same page. Since the sister had already been on property preaching, I just assumed we would be under her authority of Jesus. She decided to allow the pastor to preach the first sermon in our church, which was not Holy Ghost filled. We had a very good turnout of about twenty-five people considering it was only the first Sunday. My neighbor had prepared a wonderful dinner we served following the service. After the first service was over, the pastor's wife came up to me with a smile on her face telling me how their dreams came true of them having their own church. I was a little taken aback by her comment because the building had been empty for a long time and they were giving out bread at the same time, so why hadn't they done what we did? I had an uneasy feeling about her comment but I didn't say anything and just kept it to myself.

This first service the pastor didn't want to use the sister's sound equipment, yet brought his own as though her equipment was too small. The second and third Sundays were awesome with the sister preaching the second and me preaching the third. God's presence was in the building so thick, it was an incredible feeling. There were people falling out, getting prayed for, testifying what God had done for them, down South singing, etc. God had certainly used us to get His message to His people by their response. We were reluctant to take up offerings because we assumed the people were barely making ends meet anyway. Even with our assumption, the people still gave because they wanted to give back to Jesus.

During both of our services, I noticed a jealous reaction on the faces of the pastor and his family. I thought at the time that it was because about ninety-five percent of the people who attended, we had encouraged to attend. A friend told me that this guy passed her house when I was preaching and put out the blunt he was smoking after hearing my voice. She said he showed great interest in what he was hearing and questioned her about me. It wasn't me he was hearing, but it was really God through me.

When the pastor would preach, the people seemed bored, he would get lost in his notes, he would sort of chastise the people for their sins, he would get silent for seconds not knowing what to say, he would get the scriptures confused in the Bible, he would always talk about his misfortunes instead of those of the lost lambs listening, etc. There was so much confusion in his messages the people would hardly attend the Sundays he'd preach. Most of the ones who did attend his services only did because we were there trying to support him.

On the third Sunday there were over forty people who attended the service in that little building. Suddenly problems began to arise up over the offerings when the sister and myself decided not to take them up on our Sundays, but the pastor objected to those practices. There were a few incidents that happened with the pastor and the money that we were suspicious about and didn't approve of. There were envelopes passed through gates, over the table, during secret meetings, etc., none of which were exposed and accounted for. We even made orders of service for our designated Sundays which offerings were not part of and the pastor would still stand up at the end of service asking the people for money. The first thing he would say before requesting the offering was to tell the people the money they gave was not for him personally. It was as if he was using the money for personal obligations because the little bread and food he gave out were free. There was also a division on the church service length of time. The pastor wanted to keep the people there a really long time. Then the pastor decided to change the name of the church to "Church on the Hill" without consultation with either of us, even though God had confirmed our name through my neighbor. He also changed the "order of service" demanding we use his, which was longer, integrated his family much more participation, still had an offering slated, and was very disorganized in its format. His practices were totally against the visions God had given my sister and me, and we were not going to be part of it. We decided not to participate in any of the services because it caused too much confusion.

One thing is that the spirit has to be there in order for people to continue coming back. They go for changes in their lives and if they come out of church the same, they won't be eager to return because they won't have the hunger to be fed. They were starving in the streets and when they did eat, they were given the wrong food, yet tired of never getting full. The seeds that were planted long ago in their lives have the appetite for good food and not the junk food they've been getting anywhere. Selfishness and greed will try to steal God's visions and make them their own. When God gives someone a vision, it's that person's vision for him/her to perform a duty for God's purpose. Flesh cannot take their vision and use it for its own purpose, but they can help the other reach the vision God gave them. Many times, including our experience, flesh will allow others who run with God's vision to set up everything, then come out with God giving them the same vision. If God had really given them the same vision, they were either disobedient or realized there's something good happening and wanted to take advantage for their own personal gain. There's a big difference between God's visions and fleshly dreams.

The pastor said that God had given him the same vision as the sister, yet he waited until we had set the church up to expose his vision. He told us God had told him to pastor a church on property, but never did anything about it, even with the same building sat empty for almost all of the time he had been on property. The question becomes why hadn't he already used the closed building and set up his church even before we came along? When he replaced our small sound system with his larger one wasn't the problem because it would be louder and maybe someone far off could hear the messages? The problem was that our system wasn't good enough to fit his, not God's, status. What he forgot was that if God can hear silent prayers from us, no matter which system used, the people He sent to hear would hear. Jesus didn't use any sound system in His days and His Words sounded off to multitudes. Always remember, if God is using you to send out His Word, it will get to the intended ones, but if God isn't using you, then maybe you'll need a larger sound system. The bottom line is, they won't hear you anyways, large or small.

God uses us to get His message to someone and that person will know something is different. You can just out of the blue turn on the TV, read a writing, hear a word from a stranger, etc., and hear a word that pertains to the issue you are going through at that moment. It will immediately summon your attention that there is a connection. You can be in church and the preacher says something or references the sermon title that you will feel like he/she is personally speaking to you. All of which, God is sending a message to you through a worldly means. Sometimes it's not what we want to hear and try to avoid the direct message because it doesn't feel good, but you know deep down in your heart it was for you. Even if you ignore it, you cannot forget about it because you know it is the truth and sometimes, God will send the same message through some other means back to you. Offerings are received to help build God's kingdom and to be available for ones in need, not to line preachers' pockets for personal gain. God will supply all, not just some of our needs, which indicate He will bless us with enough to take care of our own and others' needs. If your motive is wrong in asking for offerings, then, you shouldn't ask, especially if you're putting your personal obligations over the needs of God's people. God blesses us to bless others. When people have to defend themselves without being asked about the spending of God's money, they are guilty about something they did ungodly with previous money. A thief will always tell you he/she is stealing from you if you listen closely enough. Their guilt will make them think someone knows, even if the people listening have no idea. People don't defend themselves if nothing is wrong because they have nothing to defend. Our biggest problem most times is putting money before God and if our mission is "of God," He already has the financial end worked out. When all of those people came to our little church, it wasn't us that filled the room, yet it was God's true words. Satan will be on the outside, by the front door, or the inside of a church if he is invited in or the church is divided. The Bible says a house divided cannot stand. This pastor wasn't going against us in the flesh, rather going against God's will. It wasn't about us anyway, yet about establishing a kingdom for God's lost lambs. My sister and I separated ourselves because of the confusion knowing that Satan is the author of confusion with full knowledge we weren't going to be a part of Satan's works.

After we separated from the church we started, we decided to call a meeting with the property manager and the pastor. All we wanted was our equal share of the room on Sundays. It was our intention for the manager to alternate each Sunday between us all because we felt that was the only fair way. Before the meeting with the manager, we met several times on the grounds of the property to see if we could work our problems out. Our last meeting was the most shocking because the pastor told the sister for the first time that God had told him to be the pastor over the whole property and church. He also said that if he had hurt the sister in any way, he would walk away from the property. He could tell she was hurting then, but he didn't walk off. He also bragged about his papers ordaining him as a pastor, insinuating by us not having any papers, he had priority and authorization over us.

I got up from the meeting, left them still sitting there, and walked home because I knew then there would be no compromise. We agreed to give it one last chance to work. We sat through his service the following week and got ready for ours the next week. The sister had another obligation and she asked me to preach on her behalf using our program.

Right before that Sunday, I ran into the pastor who was coming from somewhere on property and asked me about the program. I told him we were going to use our own but I felt then he was going to wait until Sunday and try to change things. He knew the sister wasn't going to be there because of her other engagement already scheduled. One of my sons who came into town wanted to go to church with me and hear me preach, which was a highlight in my life.

The first thing that Sunday morning after all of the people had assembled, the pastor called me outside and told me to go by his agenda instead of ours. I refused, telling him he had to do everything except the message and I would do only that. I didn't want to make a scene, especially with my son in attendance. We went back inside of the building and the pastor picked up all of our agendas passing out his own, which disturbed some of our followers. I allowed him to do his part, I did mine, and we ended the service. My sermon touched my son so much, he gave his life to Jesus and that touched me deeply. We decided after what had just happened, we could no longer work with the pastor and asked for a meeting with the property manager.

When we got into the meeting after both sides presented their schedules, the manager told us we had to work with him and he had priority over the property. She told us if we couldn't work with him, we needed to find someplace else to have our church. The pastor even came onto my porch and spoke with the sister and me, informing us that anything spiritual happening on the property had to come through him. He also said that I was not a man of God. I stayed calm until he said that and that's when I blew up at him, even though it showed me his ignorance. I told him no man has authority over me and that my authority came from God. This pastor didn't even live out on the property, nor did he make frequent visits. How would he know what these residents' hurts were? How was he to tell anyone he had to approve how he/she served God, especially being a state-funded property? He even told the sister that he was on property first, but everyone knew she was the first one.

We separated ourselves totally even down to the chairs the sister had brought in. God gave the sister the word earlier when we tried to work with the pastor, to let the weeds and stares grow together and He, not us, would separate them. Afterwards, we were invited to have our service at this other church, but all of a sudden, that became a problem with time, cost, contract, etc. Of course, that didn't surprise me because after attending a couple of their services, I wasn't impressed because of its non-growth, non-spirit-filled atmosphere, "better than thou" attitude, and all of the things that would draw the lost to membership. You could tell there was no one acting as a disciple in the large neighborhood that surrounded their church. My sister even asked a brother from this church to conduct her Bible study lessons each Tuesday and after he listened to the property pastor who conned him into conducting them each week, he questioned her vision from God. When he first started, he felt the same as what the pastor showed us, so he knew the pastor wasn't right from the beginning. I personally heard this man and he submitted himself under my sister's authority, telling her whatever she wanted him to do, he'd do. He saw an opportunity for himself, took advantage of the pastor's weakness, and wouldn't stand up for what was obvious. I believe both of these men had a problem with the sister because they didn't believe a female should have any authority. The church of the brother who taught Bible study was dominated with female authorities, which he probably resented and wanted his so-called proper place.

The pastor hadn't succeeded in preaching at his home church, getting enough people interested in his property bread ministry, feeding the property kids because the state stopped funding, and different events scheduled to be held on property (movie night, kids' programs, etc.), so he certainly wasn't going to let this opportunity pass him by. When would you notice there was something wrong and maybe God didn't tell you to do all of those things? When do you realize reality or do you just continue to scatter the sheep with your personal dreams and not God's will? When do you realize that God maybe only wants you to be a follower and not a leader? When do you realize you can't get respect unless you earn respect? When do you realize you can't steal the authority that God gave to someone else just because of personal status? When do you finally realize it's not going to work because you're putting your own selfishness before God and His lost sheep?

We can't serve two masters, either we serve God or we serve Satan and the choice is up to us. Many people perpetrate God on the outside and have a heart of Satan on the inside. We want to portray Jesus making people feel we really care about them, we're there to serve the lost, we believe and live by what we preach, etc., when most if not all of it is far from the truth. Many times as soon as they leave our sights, we talk down about them, laugh/joke about them, start rumors about them, or take part in other negative behaviors trying to make ourselves look good. We may fool the people, but we don't fool God because He knows our hearts.

Some people think that a piece of paper that man gave them gives them authority. Anyone, even the lost souls, can have his/her names typed in on a piece of paper and get someone else to sign it. It's only a piece of paper if God didn't ordain us. Many of those papers are given to preachers, ministers, deacons, etc., because of likes, compassion, gifts, or any other reasons that are not of God. A piece of paper doesn't excite me, but the Jesus in you does. A degree, an award, or any other likeness cannot lead the lost to Jesus, but it takes a pure inner heart.

When the above pastor told the sister he would leave the property if he hurt her and didn't leave after hurting her, it was nothing but a lie. If he lies in your face, how are you going to trust him with anything, especially God's lost souls? Lies for compassion only introduce deception and mistrust. Power doesn't come from man rather it comes from the will of God. We have a lot of power-hungry Christians who will use their manmade authority to get ahead, mostly for self-gain. They will copy others with better ideas than theirs (of course, the others got theirs from God), but if you notice, both ideas are almost identical. This is how the above property pastor got the name of his church, order of service, and special functions for the residents. Even in the midst of confusion, if God has a message through His vessel, His Words will get out and not come back void. That's what happened when my son gave his life to Jesus after I delivered the message. God's Word got to him even in the midst of all of the confusion that went on. When the property manager wasn't fair and sided with the pastor, she wasn't being unfair to us, but she was being unfair to God. She chose to give man all of the authority and not God, even forcing God's vision to work with Satan or nothing. She claimed to be a Christian woman, but she was certainly blinded by Satan. When she told us to go somewhere else, she was telling God to leave. How do people expect to last when they totally shut out God from His lost lambs? How are you going to fight against God and His visions and win? Your loss may not come in a day, week, month, or year, but you will lose. When God, not man, sets up a vision, He gives everything you need and moves out anything standing in the way of fulfilling His purpose. It will always work if God said to do it, but won't if man is doing it in Jesus' name and He was no part of it. This is what happened to the property pastor. He tried to give away bread and at one point, was about to shut it down because of non-participation. If you get all of this bread, fruits, ice creams, medicines, cakes, pies, vegetables, etc., from a center that donates all of it, then why don't you give it all to the people in need? Why do they have to go to your church services to get any of it? Why do you put all of it out letting the people get what they want rather than rationing or holding back certain items? What happened to all of the ice cream, fruits, vegetables, etc., picked up but not displayed? Why would you wonder why your bread ministry is failing? He tried to feed lunches and dinners to the kids and lost funding from the state, then stopped completely because of no donations/participation. He tried to show movies to the residents on a particular night each week and had to stop because of non-participation. He tried to schedule fun and games night and that never got off of the ground. He tried to do holiday feedings and got low turnouts with hardly any of the regular residents attending. Many times he would try to bribe or buy the residents in order for them to attend his church services. You can't buy or bribe someone a way to heaven, nor will just attending his services get them there. When things open and shut like the above, it simply means that God is not a part of them. God would've had the people waiting in line for each of those occasions because they would've been drawn to Him and not man or the occasion. It's simple, if you keep trying and nothing is working, you need to look at self and question whether God told self to do it in the first place. Many of us want self-glory so bad, we would never ask that question and continue to deceive ourselves. We certainly won't conclude that maybe God didn't call us to do the job we're trying to accomplish.

If we are persistent in our ungodly visions, God will take His hand off of us and allow us to continue until we fall. He'll allow us to get so high thinking we're almost there before the bottom falls from under us. We are so self-righteous and so blind we don't even see it coming, especially if it's a slow process of falling. When we finally realize it, it will be too late, then, we have to call on God in a very fervent way. A fervent prayer of a righteous man availeth much! The sad thing is that the followers who know and still choose to follow because of their selfishness will also fall.

Another thing that's bad is when a supposed church of God offers an answer for your needs because of trying to look good at the time, then, puts all kinds of obstacles consistently in your face. It would've been better if they never offered. Many times this behavior comes from fear of better results. They don't really realize how many blessings they would have received if they only obeyed God and not turned their backs on, not us, but Him. Double-minded people invite confusion and selfishness. Satan wants you to be double-minded because he can hold on to all of those he already has serving him. Where do we get the idea that God won't use a female to spread His Word? Why do so many males have this problem? What we are really saying is that the Bible was only written for males to read and tell about. The dictionary defines the word disciple as "one" who accepts and assists in spreading the doctrines of another. Disciple also means "one" of Christ's followers. It doesn't say male or female, yet it says "one." Go into all of the world and spread My gospel.

Many of the unmarried female Christians are only married to Jesus, so whom do they submit to? Is it all men, all males with church authority and if so, does it mean those males come before Jesus, especially if the women don't have an earthly husband? On those women who are married, are they to submit to a husband when man, not God, joined them in marriage? How many preachers, ministers, etc., have signed marriage certificates that are not ordained by God? Did God join that marriage together or did man do it for a price? Females have a direct line to Jesus just like the males and He talks to them as well as He talks to the males. Again, why is there only a male authority? Women are counted as "one" separate spirit in God's eyes. I believe that "women not spreading the word in an authority capacity" is manmade. We're all disciples of Christ no matter what title we hold and our job is to get lost souls to know about Christ, have a personal relationship with Him, and instruct them how to get saved. Both Christian genders have that responsibility, not just the males. My sister is well within her right to stand firm on her position, not to worry about man's interpretation, and continue spreading the word in whatever capacity God, not man, ordains her. We forget God sets our stages and sends the wounded to us for encouragement from Him. Why would He do that to females if He had a problem with it?

Due to all that had happened with the unfair treatment, my sister and I could've gone to the apartment's higher authorities, but we didn't. Surely we could have filed complaints on racial and religious discrimination, and we probably would have won. The property manager was clearly in violations of HUD and the inner apartment laws. We decided that God had brought us that far and He was the One who gave us the vision, so we agreed to allow God to continue taking care of it. It was very hard to let go on something we were part of building, especially when we would see the lost souls slip backwards or others asking when we would take over again. They had tried the pastor's services, but didn't return because they said they didn't feel anything (no change). Even with the church separation, the porch ministry continued and is still continuing at this writing. The property management feared the porch ministry because nothing changed after they treated us so unfairly. The people were still gathering on the porch and the property office had a straight view of it. They thought that all rumors, fights, etc., were stemming from the porch gathering because they had to use that as an excuse, really not knowing what was going on around them.

The property management all of a sudden began to physically support every function the pastor was having, yet had never supported my sister in any of her functions throughout any of the years. After a few weeks, the membership in the pastor's church started dropping, property crime began to increase, the communication between the residents and pastor started declining, and talk about the church became non-existent, Bible study participants began to decline, and all of the symptoms caused a slow death to the pastor's ungodly vision. A little later, the property manager was terminated and most of the ones who supported the pastor were moved to other properties. The pastor and his family still don't get what is happening to them, yet they still try to hold on to this obvious false vision. They even tried to put up a large church service sign and sent three people to try to invite me back. Now, the pastor had told me that I wasn't a man of God, which made me as a servant to Satan, so why would he want someone as ungodly as me to participate in his ministry? That in itself said that his motives weren't right from the start and what he was doing was of flesh, not of God. How can you be property pastor when you're not on property regularly talking to all of the people finding out what their hurts and needs are?

Sometimes we have to give it to Jesus and let Him handle it, especially when every time we try, we mess it up. If we truly believe He told us to do something and it doesn't go the way we expect it to go, then we must believe that it's His purpose to allow the obstacles. We must remove our hands off of the situation and allow God to do His work because He knows the ending. He who waits on the Lord shall renew his strength! Our ways are not His ways! Sometimes we feel that we know more than God and we can do things better than Him. If we really believe that God guides our footsteps, then we have to trust Him enough to know that He separates us because the ending is better for us. His reason may be to get us totally away so He can do what He needs to do to the perpetrator and his/her followers. He doesn't want them to fault anyone but himself/herself. It doesn't mean that our visions we got from God won't be fulfilled, yet all of His actions are in His plan. We have to submit because our battles aren't ours, but they are the Lord's. We need to stay away, not interfere, and allow God to do His job. Satan can have us so deceived he'll have us imagining visions that are not even there. We'll be so sensitive to fear, we'll make the righteous our enemies of blame. Nothing working certainly won't be caused by us, yet it's so easy to always put the blame on others. We always feel that everyone is out to take our vision away from us. God will remove our main source of flesh protection causing us to be out there alone slowly dying.

With the property manager terminated and the property pastor not increasing, God was letting the dead bury the dead. That's one of the reasons God didn't want us to file a complaint on the property manager. Reprobation will have us so confused, we won't see our life dying before our own eyes, yet always using the phrase "it's getting better." There were many lost sheep in the house when we were there and the pastor has scattered them back into the wilderness. Woe unto the shepherd who scatters my sheep! When flesh finally starts seeing that there's something wrong, it's normally too late, causing desperation. We tend to forget about the ones we badly talked about, shut out, thought not good enough, etc., when things, we think, are going good. Yet we call on those same ones when things go bad to bail us out. All of a sudden, those same ones are good enough and not as bad as originally thought because of desperation. The pastor wanted "ole no-good me" because he knew my followers would increase his few to many. I refused and declined his invitation because I would never expose my lost sheep or myself to a knowing wrong. Their blood would be on my hands and I would have to answer for them not getting the right food.

We must be careful when we advertise churches to the lost sheep we minister to because of their vulnerable conditions. We don't want them to be hurt any more than they already hurt. You can put neon signs on each corner and on top of a building, but if the Holy Spirit isn't there, the people won't come. Those who do elect to try it out won't stay because what they need is not there. Sometimes they would even shut down the church for personal reasons leaving those lost sheep stranded. If it is God's house, how can you shut down and not find a way to keep the doors open? That is equivalent to closing the doors on or shutting out God.

When Peter began to sink after walking on the water, he called out to Jesus for help and not Satan. Sometimes we're too proud to call on Jesus even when the water is over our heads. We feel we're a good enough swimmer to get ourselves out, yet that's how so many of us drown. Jesus immediately stretched out His hand and saved Peter telling him, "O ye of little faith."

I remember one day right after church, this little four-year-old boy went over to the church and asked for a dollar for his birthday. The property pastor and some of his followers were outside, then told the little boy they needed to "get out" after hunching his shoulders as to say he had no money. The little boy, his sister, and a couple more friends bicycled away from there in distress and went to tell his mother. How can anyone, especially a so-called pastor, turn his/her back on such a young child for a single dollar? What will that rejection do to those children in their futures in a relationship with pastors and churches? It seems such a small incident, yet that rejection will remain with them a long time, if not forever. We have to be extremely careful in our smallest to largest behaviors with children because they are within their future molding stages. The pastor rejected one of God's most precious creations and he will definitely have to answer for that. A wrath is a violent or extreme anger that God has for you concerning something you did that He didn't approve of. Representing ourselves in God's name with sinful or selfish motives brings on God's wrath, especially when that behavior causes the hurt to become more hurt. If we bring on a wrath of God onto ourselves,

He'll forgive us if we ask, but we still have to suffer the consequences for making Him so angry. He'll have mercy on us, but we still have to pay and most times it's when we think we're doing better that our punishment comes. Satan will have us thinking that God has forgotten and we've escaped or not acknowledged we did wrong in the first place. When it comes down, we always act surprised and start questioning why it happened. Never do we reflect back on those we hurt, especially if God has allowed us to do better than we were doing back then. God is the only One who has that schedule. Even in our punishment stage, especially then, we have to give God all of our praises because He's the only One who can end it. We have to always remember that God sends us through all bad so good will come out to help someone He sends our way in the future. We most often remember and talk about the details of the hard times than we do the good times because God wants us to understand who brought us out of our bad situations. The sad part is that many of us are so selfish we honestly believe that we brought ourselves out, not giving God any of the praise. I can do all things through Christ, not man, who strengthens me! It doesn't say I can do all things through myself because I have too many weaknesses. Again, luck shouldn't be in our vocabulary if we're truly allowing God to guide our every footstep. How are we strong enough to bring ourselves out of the valley of the shadow of death?

If we depended on our own strength, we would quickly

allow that shadow to overcome us by giving up. We'll always go through some type of trial and tribulation, but we must understand that the only way out is God. Just like God is real, we must believe that His wrath is real also. Everything we do or say, God gives us a choice to do or say the right thing even before it happens. We can either follow His Words or follow our fleshly minds and most times, we choose the easier out which isn't God's ways. Our biggest problem is when we make that wrong decision. Satan is waiting to cash in on our weakness because he sees an opportunity. The less time we give Satan, the more time we give God and less chance for His wrath.

CHAPTER TEN

CONCLUSION

A: WRITING REASONS

My reasons for writing this book were to go back and see how God has been in my life from my beginning. By writing it, my eyes have opened up to the reality of mistakes I've made throughout my life, yet understanding some would've been grave if it had not been for God's protection. It also showed me that the seed that was planted in my earlier life would remain there until it's watered and grown. It showed me how awesome God was in guiding my every footsteps. Looking back, there is an explained understanding why God allowed me to go through all of the good and all of the bad throughout my life. He was giving me experience that I would need in my later life so I could be a testimony to someone else He had waiting on me. How could I truly tell someone hurting it would be fine if I hadn't lived through the same and came out by God's grace? I had to put my experiences in writing because others need to read how good God really is, especially if they are going through the things I've been through. Sharing my experiences will, hopefully, increase others' faith and belief that all things happen for reasons with their only out being God. It also defines God's undeniable love He has for each and every one of us, especially when we fall into the grips of Satan serving him more than God. There are so many stories in the Bible that relate to our lives of today and writing this book will show some of those connections. It also showed me that God really does know our futures and began preparing us for each step at birth.

B: GOD AND SATAN—FIFTY-THREE YEARS

It is absolutely true that Satan can only do to us what God allows him to do. Satan is deceitful, conniving, sly, slick, selfish, jealous, envious, and much more to use against our weaknesses only for his glory. Satan will expose himself at our weakest moments knowing that we don't have the strength to fight against him. One of the things that Satan doesn't know about is the limit he can push us to because God holds our ultimate futures. Satan will also trick us into thinking many of our thoughts come from God, even in the backs of our minds we have a question of its authenticity. Most likely, if we have to question, it's not from God because He will set the obvious stage without doubt. Satan will use our own emotional and fleshly goals for his own benefit because he knows all of the sin we have to adopt in order to reach them. He will set in front of us what we like, how we like it, and give us a false belief of it being created just for us. Satan knows if we want it bad enough, we'll allow him to guide us, thus forgetting about God. He'll keep us so preoccupied that we won't have the time to think whether our actions are of God. Even after Satan has taken us to our limit and God brings us out, he's still hanging around waiting for us to make our next mistake during our weakness. Anyone who thinks Satan ever gives up is only fooling himself/herself, especially when we give our lives to Christ. Anytime we try to uplift God, especially to Satan's followers, he gets angry and causes a close disturbance to interrupt that gathering. He knows if we plant a seed of God's Word, his chance of holding onto them becomes very slim. It seemed easier to follow the fun rules of Satan rather than follow the strict rules of God, even knowing the outcomes were much different (wouldn't last with Satan, but would last with God). Out of all of those years, I'm certainly glad God had more authority than Satan because I wouldn't be here to write this book. God was and still is a forgiving God. There is no doubt that God has been watching over me since my beginning and the stories in this book prove that fact.

C: THE REALNESS

The people in this book are real and the incidents are true to the best of my memory. God has been with me and guided me throughout the writing of this book. I've never gone to college for writing lessons, but I can certainly write about the goodness of God throughout my life thus far. We don't have to graduate from a college to tell those stories. If these things have happened to me, they have happened or are happening to others. This book is of truth and if I've stepped on anyone's toes, I'm not sorry because there are too many covering up the real truth of God. They're stuck in their little shells of same, not wanting anyone else in to expose that they have problems stumbling and falling just like the rest of us. There's much too much fakeness and false prophesy in our spiritual sect that is keeping the confused more confused. We don't understand that not being real is making Satan more powerful and much more available to deceive us into believing our unreal is real. If we are deceived, we won't call upon the Lord for understanding, yet continue to lean on our own. This also makes us vulnerable to accept and believe any false prophesy anyone tells us. Many of us know the truth, but have allowed our political ambitions or sinful motives to keep our mouths shut and dictate our wrong behaviors. We may hide our realness from other flesh, but we certainly can't hide it from God and He's the only One who matters.

D: GOD IS THE ANSWER

God is the only One who knows your beginning and

your ending, along with everything in between. All He asks from us is to spend a little time with Him and develop a personal relationship with Him, thus allowing Him to come into our lives. In all of my ups and downs, God was the only One I could depend on and always was there when I needed him. There hasn't been nor will there ever be any flesh to stick by me as close as God. There hasn't been nor will there ever be anyone who will love me as much as He does. Friends, relatives, etc., will show love, but it's compromising, whereas God's love is uncompromising. God said, ask and ye shall receive, seek and ye shall find, knock and the door will be open! Even throughout all of my sin, God was still with me and that's much more than I can say for any of my fleshly associates. Most of them, if not all, were there when I was up, but didn't stick around when I was down. It was almost up to this writing when I realized I could have a personal relationship with the One who created me and He would take care of me and all of my needs. I tried Him with nothing, not knowing I had everything all along and all I had to do was ask. I don't even have to worry about where I walk because He guides all of my steps and if it's not good for me, He'll block off that path. I don't have to worry about all the dangers that surround me because He's built a hedge of protection around me to follow me wherever I go. He makes my enemies my footstools and all I have to do is stand back, allowing Him to fight my battles. I never worry about being hungry or thirsty because, not only does he provide for my earthly body, I eat from His Word and drink from His living water. With Him, I'm full all of the time and He feeds me "till I want no more." He has proven to me that we can live just on faith and belief as long as we're trying to walk with Him. God will never leave or forsake you! He is my only answer.